RUN

like a

GIRL

RUN like a GIRL

Danielle Brown

Button
Books

CONTENTS

Turning Ordinary 6
into Extraordinary

Run *like a* Girl 8
Allyson Felix

Catch *like a* Girl 10
Sarah Taylor

Brave *like a* Girl 12
Bethany Hamilton

Defy the Rules *like a* Girl 14
Maria Toorpakai

Lead a Team *like a* Girl 16
Kate Richardson-Walsh

Drive *like a* Girl 18
Susie Wolff

Break Records *like a* Girl 20
Hannah Cockroft

Have Skills *like a* Girl 22
Liv Cooke

Paddle *like a* Girl 24
Lizzie Carr

Kind *like a* Girl 26
Nikki Hamblin

Tough *like a* Girl 28
Lynne Cox

Win *like a* Girl 30
Simone Biles

Box *like a* Girl 32
Nicola Adams

Pave the Way *like a* Girl 34
Manon Rhéaume

Dance *like a* Girl 36
Misty Copeland

Climb Mountains *like a* Girl 38
Arunima Sinha

Coach *like a* Girl 40
Tracey Neville

Throw *like a* Girl 42
Dame Valerie Adams

Try *like a* Girl 44
Maggie Alphonsi

Race *like a* Girl 46
Jasmin Paris

Ski *like a* Girl 48
Menna Fitzpatrick

Score *like a* Girl 50
Marta Vieira da Silva

Dare to Dream *like a* Girl 52
Yusra Mardini

Cycle *like a* Girl 54
Dame Laura Kenny

Jump *like a* Girl 56
Mariya Lasitskene

Inspire *like a* **Girl**
Sarah Williams
58

Swing *like a* **Girl**
Shanshan Feng
60

Row *like a* **Girl**
Heather Stanning
62

Climb *like a* **Girl**
Sasha DiGiulian
64

Beat the Odds *like a* **Girl**
Novlene Williams-Mills
66

Ride *like a* **Girl**
Sophie Christiansen
68

Succeed *like a* **Girl**
Dame Jessica Ennis-Hill
70

Skate *like a* **Girl**
Sky Brown
72

Swim *like a* **Girl**
Natalie du Toit
74

Fence *like a* **Girl**
Valentina Vezzali
76

Sail *like a* **Girl**
Dame Ellen MacArthur
78

Cross the Finish *like a* **Girl**
Kathrine Switzer
80

Explore *like a* **Girl**
Karen Darke
82

Stand Out *like a* **Girl**
Tamika Catchings
84

Fight *like a* **Girl**
Katheryn Winnick
86

Referee *like a* **Girl**
Stéphanie Frappart
88

Play *like a* **Girl**
Serena Williams
90

Multitalented *like a* **Girl**
Oksana Masters
92

Push My Limits *like a* **Girl**
Chrissie Wellington
94

Strong *like a* **Girl**
Lydia Valentín
96

Joust *like a* **Girl**
Sarah Hay
98

Rise to the Top *like a* **Girl**
Saina Nehwal
100

Adventure *like a* **Girl**
Mollie Hughes
102

Slide *like a* **Girl**
Lizzy Yarnold
104

Be the Best *like a* **Girl**
Rachel Atherton
106

About *the* **Author**
Danielle Brown
108

Index
110

TURNING ORDINARY *into* EXTRAORDINARY

"You run like a girl!"

If you ever hear these words it's time to smile and put on your game face. Stand a little taller and a little prouder.

They are right.

You are strong and brave and fierce. Like a girl.

You are ambitious and resilient and tough. Like a girl.

You can run like a girl, catch like a girl, and throw like a girl. You can dream like a girl and win like a girl.

There are so many amazing women around the world, shattering records and breaking through barriers. Every day they show talent, tenacity, and tireless commitment, redefining outdated stereotypes and delivering some breathtaking performances.

These women started out just like you or me. They went on to achieve some extraordinary things because they believed in their dreams and didn't let anything get in their way.

Just remember: there is no dream too big or goal too high. If you want it badly enough, if you work hard enough, and if you choose to get back up every time you are knocked down, then you will find yourself in a world without limits.

This book introduces you to 50 female athletes, each with a different story to tell. They come from across the globe, and do completely different sports. You will see the pinnacles of human performance and adaptability. The fierce competitors and comeback queens, the thrill seekers, change makers, and barrier breakers. From start to finish, no story is the same, and yet a common thread runs through each one: passion.

Passion is the driving force behind action. It motivates us to turn up each day prepared to give maximum effort. There are no shortcuts to success, and these athletes deliver awesome results because they work so hard to achieve them. They don't care how much time it takes to get better. They understand what can be accomplished if they strive for better every single day. It fuels their determination to hang in there when it gets tough and others walk away in defeat.

Every athlete has experienced obstacles on their path to success. There were doubters who told them they couldn't do it. They made huge sacrifices to get good at their sport, and pushed through frustrating dips in performance. They kept on going because their drive was stronger than the negatives. They stayed curious, remained relentlessly positive, and rose to meet challenges head on.

Think about what your passions are. You might not know yet and that's okay. Some of the athletes in this book tried loads of sports before they discovered the one for them, some came across theirs by accident, and some talents were spotted by others. There is a sport out there for everyone and it can take time for a hobby to blossom into something that fires us with excitement and ambition.

We are not born with our future already decided, it is something we must write for ourselves. Your journey to success begins with enthusiasm. When you find a purpose that is bigger than you, when you back it up with hard work and choose to believe in your goals, then you start to transform an ordinary beginning into something extraordinary. Don't let anybody else define your passions, but stay true to your dream. And remember, there is no limit to your potential.

RUN *like a* GIRL
Allyson Felix

Full name: **Allyson Michelle Felix**
Sport: **Athletics**
Birth date: **November 18, 1985**
Place of birth: **Los Angeles, USA**
Team: **USA**
Best achievement: **The most decorated track athlete ever (male or female!) with 30 global championship medals**

Did you know...?

★ Allyson is the most successful athlete at World Championship level. With 14 golds, she has even more medals than Usain Bolt.

★ She is a powerful activist for women in sport. Nike wanted to pay her 70% less in sponsorship money after she had a baby. Allyson challenged this, leading to a big shake up in how female athletes are treated.

★ Allyson has a degree in elementary education from the University of Southern California and has spoken of wanting to be a teacher.

In the world of athletics Allyson Felix is a superstar. With eleven Olympic medals (seven of them gold) she is one of the fastest people on the planet. Her personal best for the 200m sprint is 21.69 seconds, which is phenomenally quick!

Allyson tried out for the running team at school and she came seventh in her first race. Her times improved quickly and soon she was winning state meets, but she was told that her legs were too long and spindly for her to be a good runner. Powering her way to success again and again, Allyson proves that you don't have to have a specific body shape to become a world-class athlete.

She was 18 when she competed at her first Olympics, Athens 2004. Allyson won the silver medal in the 200m race, breaking the world junior record. A year later she became the youngest sprinter to take the World Championship title. Her first Olympic gold medal came in Beijing 2008 in the 4x400m relay team, and in London 2012 she became the second female track and field athlete to win three gold medals in a single Games.

After such an amazing performance you might expect a repeat at the 2013 World Championships, but a hamstring injury meant she missed out on a medal. This was the first time she had left a World Championships without a medal. Allyson fought back and despite further injuries she won two golds and a silver at Rio 2016.

Being the best in the world doesn't mean that you jump from glittering golds to sparkling silvers without experiencing setbacks. It's about pushing on in spite of them. In 2018 Allyson faced a huge obstacle. When she was 32 weeks pregnant with her daughter Camryn she was rushed to hospital with a life-threatening condition, and her baby was delivered by emergency caesarean section. Surgery like this puts your body under a tremendous amount of strain and requires a long recovery period, but ten months later Allyson won her 12th and 13th gold medals at the World Championships in Doha. At the Tokyo 2020 Olympics she won gold and bronze, making her America's most decorated track and field Olympian.

"I WILL GIVE MORE TODAY THAN I DID YESTERDAY."

TCH *a*
ah Tayl

Full name: **Sarah Jane Taylor**
Sport: **Cricket**
Birth date: **May 20, 1989**
Place of birth: **London, UK**
Teams: **Sussex and England**
Best achievements: **Three times ICC Women's T20I Cricketer of the Year, ICC Women's ODI Cricketer of the Year, and three-time Ashes winner**

"THE BEST THING I EVER DID WAS ADMIT IT. I CAN'T STRESS ENOUGH HOW IT HELPS TO TALK ABOUT MENTAL HEALTH."

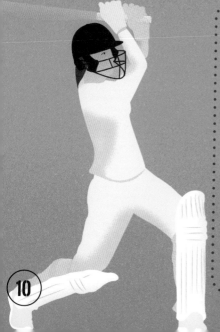

Did you know...?

★ Sarah has the highest number of international dismissals in women's cricket, dismissing 232 batters.

★ She made 226 national appearances, and after she decided to step down from the England team to look after her health, she continued to play competitively for Sussex.

★ Sarah became the first woman to be inducted into the Legends Lane at the Brighton and Hove County Cricket Ground. This award celebrates the greatest cricketers from across Sussex.

Sarah Taylor has led an incredible career of firsts, paving the way to become an influential trailblazer in the world of cricket. She is a talented batter, an extraordinary wicketkeeper, and has made some outstanding catches in her career.

Sarah burst onto the international cricket scene at just 17, playing for England. She is masterful with a bat, and spent her career smashing records. She was the youngest female cricketer to score 1,000 runs in one day internationals, and she got the highest individual score against Australia, breaking a record that had stood since 1973.

With super-quick reflexes, Sarah pulled off a lot of unbelievable catches and developed a reputation as one of the best wicketkeepers in the world. She helped England win the Ashes three times, the World Cup two times, and the World T20 title. Not only is Sarah a superstar in women's cricket, but she has been competing with males since her school days. She played for her school's first team after her head teacher recognized her talent and played her on merit. In 2015 Sarah became the first woman to play men's first-grade cricket in Australia.

What makes Sarah's story even more impressive is that throughout her career she battled with anxiety and depression. Some days this got so tough that she couldn't leave the house, so she took a break from cricket to look after her mental health. With help from doctors and her coaching team, Sarah returned to international cricket for the 2017 World Cup where she helped England win. She delivered an epic performance, setting a record with Tammy Beaumont for the highest 2nd-wicket partnership in World Cup history for women's cricket. The final was watched by over 100 million people on TV.

Sarah didn't leave cricket behind entirely when she retired from playing: she got a job as an assistant coach with the Abu Dhabi T10 league. She's the first woman to coach men's professional franchise cricket and she hopes this new role will inspire other young girls to say "if she can do it, why can't I?"

BRAVE *like a* GIRL
Bethany Hamilton

Full name: **Bethany Meilani Hamilton-Dirks**
Sport: **Surfing**
Birth date: **February 8, 1990**
Place of birth: **Hawaii, USA**
Team: **USA**
Best achievement: **First place Surf N Sea Pipeline Women's Pro**

Did you know...?

★ Bethany went to Thailand to work with orphans affected by the 2004 tsunami. She encouraged them not to be afraid of the water and inspired many to take up surfing.

★ The surfboard that Bethany was using when she was attacked by a shark is on display in the California Surf Museum. There is a shark-bite chunk missing from it.

★ Bethany's life story has been turned into a movie called *Soul Surfer*. Bethany worked as a surfing stunt double for her character.

Bethany Hamilton's story is one of immense bravery, resilience, and heart. She refused to let a life-altering accident crush her dreams of becoming a professional surfer and her persistent positivity has enabled her to become one of the best in the world.

In 2003, Bethany, then 13, was surfing at Tunnels Beach, Hawaii, when she was bitten by a 14ft (4.3m) tiger shark. Her left arm was severed just below her shoulder and she lost 60% of her blood. She was rushed to hospital where doctors managed to save her life, but there was nothing they could do to save her arm.

Bethany did not let this destroy her passion or derail her goal to become a professional surfer. Just one month later she was back out on the water. She had to adapt her style and learn how to surf with one arm, thinking creatively to overcome the challenges she faced. With modifications to her board and technique she entered her first competition three months after the shark attack.

At 17, Bethany achieved her goal of becoming a professional surfer. This job has taken her to places all over the world, where she competes alongside able-bodied athletes. Bethany has consistently proved to be a formidable force, winning multiple titles and awards.

These include a silver medal at the ASP World Junior Championships, first place at the Surf N Sea Pipeline Women's Pro event, and third at the Fiji Women's Pro, beating world champion Stephanie Gilmore.

Bethany surfs on some of the most dangerous waves in the world. One of her most remarkable performances was when she successfully conquered a 40ft (12m) wave at Jaws, which is the nickname for a place in Maui famous for its monstrously large waves. This got her nominated for Women's Best Performance in the Big Wave Awards, and what's more impressive is that she did this only six months after giving birth to her first child.

"COURAGE DOESN'T MEAN YOU DON'T GET AFRAID. COURAGE MEANS YOU DON'T LET FEAR STOP YOU."

DEFY THE RULES *like a* GIRL
Maria Toorpakai

Full name: **Maria Toorpakai Wazir**
Sport: **Squash**
Birth date: **November 22, 1990**
Place of birth: **Karak, Waziristan, Pakistan**
Team: **Pakistan**
Best achievement: **First female player from Pakistan to win a Tour event**

Did you know...?

★ Before taking up squash Maria competed in weightlifting under the fake name Genghis Khan. She won a silver medal at the All Boys Weightlifting Championships.

★ Maria is passionate about music and has ambitions to study it.

★ She has set up the Maria Toorpakai Foundation, which uses sport and education to create opportunities for children in remote communities, helping them reach their potential.

"I WANT TO TELL GIRLS THAT FEAR IS TAUGHT. YOU ARE BORN FREE AND YOU ARE BORN BRAVE"

Maria Toorpakai is a girl who defied cultural restrictions and terrorist threats to live life on her terms and follow her dreams. She is an inspiring sportswoman who demonstrates courage, stubbornness, and an unbreakable spirit both on and off the court.

Maria was born in a mountainous tribal region in northwest Pakistan that is ruled by strict religious laws. It's a dangerous place where girls are not allowed to leave the house, go to school, or play sports. So at four years old Maria cut her hair and dressed like a boy so she could play outside.

She started to play squash when she was 12, but she had to show her birth certificate to join her local club. The secret about her identity was out and she got bullied by the other players, often leaving the club covered in bruises. But her drive paid off and Maria turned professional in 2006. She was given the Salam Pakistan Award by the president, and in 2009 she won a bronze medal at the World Junior Squash Championship.

When Maria was 16 the Taliban sent her death threats because she wore shorts and chose not to wear a veil. The Pakistan Squash Federation tried to help, providing snipers around the squash court and her home. But fearing for her safety and that of others, Maria decided it would be better to train abroad. She confined herself to her house and wrote to coaches and academies around the world, hoping one would take her on. For over three years she trained in her bedroom, hitting squash balls against the wall until the neighbors complained. Eventually one of her emails reached Jonathon Power, a world champion squash player from Canada, who was so impressed by her tenacity and talent he invited her to train at his academy in Toronto.

Now Maria is Pakistan's top female squash player and one of the top 50 in the world. She became the first female player from Pakistan to win a Tour event and a Professional Squash Association Challenger 10 event. With 83 tournaments played and 110 matches won, Maria proves there is always a way to achieve your dreams.

LEAD A TEAM *like a* GIRL
Kate Richardson-Walsh

Full name: **Kate Louise Richardson-Walsh OBE**
Sport: **Hockey**
Birth date: **May 9, 1980**
Place of birth: **Manchester, UK**
Team: **Great Britain**
Best achievement: **Olympic gold medal**

Did you know...?

★ Kate spent 13 years as team captain, making her the most capped female hockey player in British history.

★ Kate and her wife Helen became the first same-sex married couple to win gold at an Olympic Games.

★ Kate has been to four Olympic Games (Sydney, Beijing, London, and Rio). She scored 49 goals, captained 375 International matches, and won 19 major international medals.

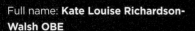

Team sports need a strong leader, and that's exactly what the Great British hockey team had in Kate Richardson-Walsh. She was instrumental in building a high-performing team, and truly understands that when you work together you can achieve so much more.

It took Kate just nine years to go from beginner to competing at her first Olympic Games. She joined a local hockey club when she was 11 and quickly moved up the ranks. Three years later she made her international debut on the under 16s team. Showing success both as a leader and a player, she was made captain at 23. Kate led the team to many wins, including bronze medals at the Commonwealth Games in Melbourne and Delhi.

At the London 2012 Olympic Games Kate was hit in the face with a hockey stick in the opening match against Japan. Great Britain went on to win 4-0, but she had to be led off the pitch with a broken jaw. This was a painful injury and could have been the end of her Olympic efforts, but after an operation she was back playing a few days later. With a metal plate in her mouth and wearing a protective face mask, Kate showed incredible grit to lead her team to a bronze medal.

Two years later Kate captained the team to a crushing defeat at the World Cup. GB arrived as favorites and left in 11th place. Kate toyed with the idea of retiring from hockey that year. The aftermath of London 2012 was tough and she questioned her passion for the sport. Deciding to take a break, Kate traveled to Hong Kong to coach juniors but returned to international hockey a few months later because she realized she had more to give. This was a great decision. In Rio 2016 she led the team to victory, winning Britain's first Olympic gold medal in hockey. In a nail-biting penalty shootout against the world number one team, the Netherlands, they delivered a historic win. Her strong performance and excellent leadership got Kate named as flag bearer, walking at the head of Team GB in the closing ceremony.

DRIVE *like a* GIRL
Susie Wolff

Ambitious, hard-working, and determined. These words sum up Susie Wolff perfectly. She carved a reputation as the fastest woman in the world, driving at speeds of over 200 miles per hour (322km/h) as a Formula One test driver.

How do you become a professional racing driver? Susie started with karting. After seeing her passion for it and an ultra-competitive streak, her parents got her a kart for her eighth birthday. In 1996, aged just 13, she was named British Woman Kart Racing Driver of the Year and held this title for four consecutive years. In 2000, she was awarded the title of Top Female Kart Driver in the World.

From karting she moved to Formula Renault, tearing around the track in a single-seater car. She made the podium three times and was nominated for the British Young Driver of the Year Award twice. Susie started a degree in international business at Edinburgh University, but as her success continued she decided to focus her efforts on driving. She moved to Silverstone in

Full name: **Suzanne Wolff MBE**
Sport: **Motorsport**
Birth date: **December 6, 1982**
Place of birth: **Oban, Argyll, UK**
Best achievement: **First woman to take part in a Grand Prix weekend in 22 years**

Did you know...?

★ Following her retirement from driving Susie joined the UK's Channel 4 as an expert analyst, reporting on Formula One racing.

★ Dare To Be Different is a grassroots initiative Susie launched to help encourage more female participation in all areas of motorsport. Susie created the platform to inspire, connect, and support girls and women.

★ Susie is the first female team principal in Formula E racing. She manages ROKiT Venturi Racing and is using her experiences in racing to lead her team to podium finishes.

"I'M NOT HERE TO BE THE BEST FEMALE. I'M HERE TO BE THE BEST."

Oxfordshire to train and poured all her energy into racing.

Her next move was Formula Three. The future was looking bright and everything was going to plan, right until she broke her ankle while running. In an unfortunate turn of events Susie then lost her sponsors and couldn't afford to pay for her spot in the World Series. This nearly put an end to Susie's career, but her many achievements had been noticed by Mercedes-Benz. They invited her to compete in DTM, the German Touring Car Championship. What started out as a one-year deal, turned into a seven-year relationship.

Her next move was into Formula One, where she was signed by Williams as a test driver. Susie was involved with the development and testing of F1 cars, ready to step up to the big stage as a reserve. With only 22 places up for grabs on the circuit, it's a tough competition with no margin for error. Susie got her wish of driving in a Grand Prix, becoming the first woman to take part in a race weekend in 22 years.

Hannah Cockroft

It is easy to understand how wheelchair racer Hannah Cockroft got the nickname Hurricane Hannah. She is an incredible athlete who crushes record after record beneath her wheels.

Shortly after Hannah was born she had two heart attacks. This caused damage to her brain and doctors said she would never walk or talk. Hannah defied these expectations and took her first steps at three years old. The brain damage caused deformities to her legs and a wheelchair helped Hannah tackle longer distances. Her goal was to become a ballerina, so she spent 13 years dancing.

Sport was trickier for Hannah to get into. At school she was initially left out by teachers who didn't know how to include her in PE lessons. It wasn't until she was 12 that her teacher Mrs Daniel introduced her to wheelchair basketball. Hannah joined a club and also tried seated discus. After winning a silver medal at the School Games she was invited to a talent day. These offer the chance to try different sports and it was here that Hannah tried wheelchair racing for the first time.

It didn't take Hannah long to get spotted by the GB team. At 18 she smashed eight world records. A year later she was invited to join the senior team, representing Great Britain at her first World Championships. She went in as an unknown and came away with two gold medals in the 100m and

> **"FIND SOMETHING YOU LOVE AND MAKE IT YOUR LIFE. THAT IS THE ONLY WAY TO BE SUCCESSFUL."**

Full name: **Hannah Lucy Cockroft MBE**
Sport: **Wheelchair racing**
Birth date: **July 30, 1992**
Place of birth: **Halifax, West Yorkshire, UK**
Team: **Great Britain**
Best achievement: **Seven Paralympic gold medals**

200m races. At the London 2012 Paralympics Hannah delivered two gold medals and two Paralympic records. She continued her unbeaten streak and in Rio 2016 she won three gold medals, retaining her 100m title, while adding the 400m and 800m to her collection. She broke Paralympic records in all three events.

Hannah continues to take the world by storm, with 12 World Championship titles under her belt. But her competitors are also improving. In 2018 she was defeated for the first time in her international career. In the face of this Hannah worked even harder and she bounced back with a world-record-breaking performance at the 2019 World Championships before winning two more golds at the Tokyo 2020 Paralympic Games.

Did you know...?

★ Hannah competes in the T34 category. In some Paralympic sports, athletes are split into different categories based on their disability. T34 is for athletes with good function in their upper body and weakness in their lower body.

★ Hannah's dance school raised money at their annual show to fund her first racing wheelchair. When it arrived it didn't fit Hannah properly so her father modified it for her.

★ Hannah has aspirations to become a TV presenter when she retires from competing. She was given a presenting slot with the BBC's *Countryfile* and did a super job.

HAVE SKILLS *like a* GIRL
Liv Cooke

Liv Cooke showcases talent, passion, and fighting spirit in a way that is simply captivating. She has managed to turn adversity into accomplishment, embracing setbacks to become the youngest freestyle soccer world champion.

Liv has always been mad about soccer. Her older brothers taught her how to play and they practiced together every night. Liv joined the local girl's team as a winger when she was ten, and by 14 she had signed with Blackburn Rovers FC. She had the drive, the talent, and the work ethic to make it to the top, but a recurring back injury forced her to take some time out. It was during her recovery that Liv came across freestyle soccer.

Freestylers can use every part of their body to perform tricks with a ball and in competitions athletes are judged on the originality, ability, difficulty, control, and execution of their routine. After watching videos online Liv was hooked and she started to learn tricks at home. She thought this would help her ball control while she was recovering from her injury and couldn't train on the pitch. Liv kept at it until she was able to pull off some awesome moves. She now had a tough decision to make. Training in one sport takes up a huge amount of time but trying to balance two was just impossible. Liv had to decide which she wanted more: to become a world champion freestyler or play soccer for England. She chose freestyling, becoming the first woman in the UK to turn pro.

The 2016 World Championships started brilliantly for Liv. At 17 she was the youngest person to qualify for this event and she made it through to the finals. So far so good, but in the finals Liv broke her foot. She hobbled away with second place. Having to take six months out to recover made Liv hungrier than ever to push forward to world number one. She spent a lot of time poring over video performances and when she was allowed to train again she worked mercilessly hard. It paid off and a year later she became the youngest ever world champion.

Did you know...?

★ After seeing videos of 15-year-old Liv doing soccer tricks on YouTube, Nickelodeon invited her to take part in a freestyle competition. Liv won, battling against three boys in the final to take the title.

★ Liv travels around the world to perform at events from street festivals to soccer matches. She works as a TV presenter and as a sports reporter on Champions League Match Day.

★ Liv is passionate about inspiring girls to take part in freestyle soccer. She wants them to be better than her, not just like her.

Full name: **Liv Cooke**
Sport: **Freestyle soccer**
Birth date: **April 20, 1999**
Place of birth: **Leyland, Lancashire, UK**
Best achievement: **Youngest freestyle soccer world champion**

PADDLE *like a* GIRL
Lizzie Carr

Sport has the power to drive incredible change and nobody demonstrates this better than Lizzie Carr. Not only is she breaking records and achieving world firsts, she is also using her platform as a paddleboarder to combat plastic pollution.

Lizzie's life started out ordinarily enough. She earned a degree in English literature at university, got a good job, and worked her way up the career ladder. On paper it all looked great, but this was not the kind of life Lizzie wanted. She decided to take go traveling. Lizzie spent the next nine months hiking in China, riding horses in Mongolia, and taking the Trans-Siberian Railway through the most isolated parts of Russia.

Lizzie went to the doctor when she got home. The glands in her neck were swollen and she was given a diagnosis that she wasn't expecting: cancer. She had an operation to remove the tumor and went through radiotherapy to kill the remaining cancer cells. Doctors didn't know whether she would survive treatment and Lizzie promised that if she got a second chance she would live life on her terms and find something that gave her purpose. A year later she was given the all clear. Lizzie returned to work, falling back into a familiar routine, but she wasn't happy. This wasn't what she had survived cancer for. She resigned from her job, which was a scary decision, but it was the right thing for her.

Lizzie started paddleboarding as part of her recovery from cancer. Being surrounded by nature made her feel relaxed, but she was horrified to see so much litter in the water. When she saw a coot's nest made from as much plastic as twigs she realized just how much it was hurting wildlife.

Lizzie discovered that 80% of the plastic that ends up in the ocean starts inland and is carried down rivers to the sea. She wanted to do something about this, so she paddled the length of England to raise awareness. She covered 400 miles (644km) in 22 days and photographed every piece of plastic she saw, tagging its location on an interactive map. She returned to some of the worst affected areas in a 'trash raft' to clear them.

"ASK YOURSELF WHAT MATTERS TO YOU IN LIFE."

Full name: **Elizabeth Carr**
Sport: **Paddleboarding**
Place of birth: **Surrey, UK**
Best achievements: **Three world firsts and founder of a worldwide environmental movement, Planet Patrol**

Did you know...?

★ Lizzie became the first woman to paddleboard across the English Channel, taking seven hours and 30 minutes. Every four miles (6.4km) Lizzie took water samples to get analyzed for microplastic content.

★ Lizzie founded Planet Patrol, an organization that coordinates clean-up events worldwide. Anybody can collect trash in their local areas and log it on the app.

★ Lizzie became the first woman to paddle all 170 miles (274km) of the Hudson River, New York State, despite a hurricane making its way up the East Coast at the time.

KIND *like a* GIRL
Nikki Hamblin

Full name: **Nikki Jayne Hamblin**
Sport: **Athletics**
Birth date: **May 20, 1988**
Place of birth: **Dorchester, Dorset, UK**
Team: **New Zealand**
Best achievement: **Two-time Commonwealth Games silver medalist**

Did you know...?

★ The Fair Play Award Nikki received has only been given 19 times in the history of the Olympics.

★ Abbey and Nikki have kept in touch since their race in Rio, and Abbey has even visited Nikki in New Zealand.

★ Nikki went to Millfield School in England, which had an amazing eight former students competing at the Rio 2016 Olympics. As well as Nikki, this included the gold medalist rowing team of Helen Glover and Heather Stanning.

At the heart of the Olympics sits three values: excellence, respect, and friendship. Middle-distance runner Nikki Hamblin displayed all three when she sacrificed precious seconds to help another competitor.

Nikki was born in the UK and she was a competitive junior, running for Dorchester Athletics Club. She moved to New Zealand when she was 18, and she switched allegiances when she was granted New Zealand citizenship in 2009. A year later she won two silver medals for New Zealand at the Commonwealth Games in Delhi in the 800m and 1500m races. Nikki was hoping to race in the London 2012 Olympics but an injury ruled her out. A long and painful recovery saw Nikki make an awesome comeback where she placed fifth at the 2014 Commonwealth Games in Glasgow.

Nikki is best known for her outstanding sportsmanship in Rio 2016. With four laps to go in the 5000m heats she tumbled to the ground. With her went the runner from the USA, Abbey D'Agostino. Their competitors kept running and didn't look back. Abbey was the first to her feet and she reached out to help Nikki up, encouraging her to finish the race. There was no real hope of catching up, but Nikki and Abbey kept on running. Abbey fell for a second time and it was clear that she had badly injured her leg. Instead of carrying on with the race, Nikki stopped to pull Abbey to her feet and waited to check she was well enough to keep racing before she continued.

Both Nikki and Abbey crossed the finish line, but did not make the qualifying time for the finals. They submitted protests to officials and were granted spots in the final. Nikki finished in 17th place and Abbey was unable to compete because of the severity of her injury. They were both presented the IOC's Fair Play award for displaying exemplary human spirit and selflessness.

"THERE'S ALWAYS A POSITIVE IN EVERYTHING."

TOUGH *like a* GIRL
Lynne Cox

Full name: **Lynne Cox**
Sport: **Open-water swimming**
Birth date: **January 2, 1957**
Place of birth: **Boston, Massachusetts, USA**
Best achievement: **Completed 60 long-distance swims around the world, many of them world records**

Did you know...?

⭐ The Russians wanted to know what Lynne would need when she landed. She asked for warm clothes and a babushka. In America, a babushka is a headscarf, while in Russia it means grandmother. So the Russians greeted Lynne with dry clothes and a grandma.

⭐ Lynne was training in the ocean one day when a baby gray whale started following her. Realizing he had lost his mother, Lynne stayed with him for over five hours until she was found.

⭐ Cape Lynne Cox on Lake Baikal in Siberia is named after her. It was her starting point for a ten-mile swim across the lake.

Lynne Cox has a 45-year career of breaking records. A long-distance swimmer, she has swum in some of the world's most dangerous waters.

Lynne's swimming coach noticed she was much stronger at the end of a training session than she was at the beginning. He encouraged her to try open-water swimming so she could test her talents at longer distances. At 15 Lynne swam from England to France, breaking the women's world record by one hour and the men's by 20 minutes. Lynne went on to swim the Channel again (breaking another world record), the Cook Strait in New Zealand (she was the first woman to achieve this), and the shark-infested waters around the Cape of Good Hope in South Africa (she was the first person to do this).

Her next major challenge was swimming the Bering Strait, the 2.7 mile (4.3km) stretch of water between the USA and Russia, which was then part of the Soviet Union. The water is covered in ice for most of the year and nothing like this had ever been attempted before. At the time it was the Cold War and tensions between the United States and the Soviet Union were high.

Lynne decided to go ahead with the swim in August 1987. She was finally given permission to land on Soviet soil just two days before her attempt. Lynne was accompanied on her swim by local Inuits in walrus-skin boats and her support team, and she made the crossing in just over two hours. When she reached the shore she was warmly welcomed by a Soviet delegation. When US President Ronald Reagan and Mikhail Gorbachev, leader of the Soviet Union, signed a nuclear disarmament treaty they said that Lynne's swim helped open the border between the two nations.

In 2002 Lynne attempted to be the first person to swim one mile (1.6km) in the waters of Antarctica. She did this in her swimming costume, cap, and goggles. The currents are unchartered and the water is at 32°F (0°C), but Lynne was determined. Swimming with penguins and dodging icebergs, Lynne swam 1.22 miles (2km) in 25 minutes and her achievement was another world first.

"THERE ARE NO LIMITS ON HOW MUCH THE HEART CAN LOVE, THE MIND CAN IMAGINE, OR THE HUMAN BEING CAN ACHIEVE."

WIN *like a* GIRL
Simone Biles

Full name: **Simone Arianne Biles**
Sport: **Artistic gymnastics**
Birth date: **March 14, 1997**
Place of birth: **Columbus, Ohio, USA**
Team: **USA**
Best achievement: **Four Olympic gold medals**

Gymnastics has never seen the likes of Simone Biles before. She reigns over her competitors with gravity-defying performances and has racked up a staggering number of wins.

Simone's early childhood can only be described as difficult. Her mother struggled with drug addictions and was unable to care for her, so she was placed in foster care. For three years Simone moved from home to home until her grandparents adopted her. This gave Simone the stability, support, and love she needed.

She started gymnastics when she was six. What was supposed to be a trip to a farm turned into a visit to a gym because of the rain.

Did you know...?

★ Simone is one of the most decorated athletes in the world, winning a spectacular 25 medals at the World Championships, 19 of them gold.

★ She has four signature gymnastics moves named after her: two on the floor, one on the vault, and one on the beam.

★ Simone couldn't qualify for the London 2012 Olympic Games because she was two-and-a-half months below the minimum age of 16.

Simone was a natural and started copying the older children. One coach was so impressed that she suggested Simone took lessons.

In 2011 Simone narrowly missed out on making the national team so she started homeschooling to increase her training. Missing out on time with friends at school was tough, but she was motivated by the goal of representing her country. It paid off, and two years later she made her senior debut. However, Simone found the pressure difficult to cope with and performed badly at the US Classic, pulling out of the vault exercise. She struggled with nerves at competitions, not believing she was good enough. Working closely with a psychologist helped to build up her confidence and later that year she won two gold medals at the World Championships.

With the hopes of a nation on her at Rio 2016, she won four gold medals and a bronze, and the world expected further big things from her at Tokyo 2020. Instead, she withdrew from her first event after getting the "twisties" and finding it hard to control her body in mid-air. Her bravest move wasn't a double pike or signature backflip, but stepping away from the competition and choosing to put her own mental health first. After taking time to recover she came back to win a bronze medal on the balance beam.

"I'D RATHER REGRET THE RISKS THAT DIDN'T WORK OUT THAN THE CHANCES I DIDN'T TAKE AT ALL."

BOX *like a* GIRL
Nicola Adams

Full name: **Nicola Adams OBE**
Sport: **Boxing**
Birth date: **October 26, 1982**
Place of birth: **Leeds, West Yorkshire, UK**
Team: **Great Britain**
Best achievement: **First woman boxer to win gold at an Olympic Games**

Did you know...?

★ When Nicola won gold in Rio 2016 she became the first British boxer to successfully defend an Olympic title in 92 years.

★ Nicola has worked as an extra in TV programs, appearing in soap operas including *Coronation Street* and *Emmerdale*.

★ She is the only female boxer to have won every title available to her, becoming European, World, Commonwealth, and Olympic champion.

"EVERYONE IS BEATABLE ON THE RIGHT DAY."

Nicola Adams set her heart on becoming an Olympic champion. She achieved this twice over, but what makes her story even more remarkable is that women's boxing wasn't an Olympic sport when she set this goal.

Nicola started boxing when she was 12. Her mother had an aerobics class and couldn't get a babysitter, so Nicola went with her. There was a children's boxing class on so she joined in and loved it. When she got home all Nicola could talk about was boxing. She begged her mother to take her back.

The coach at the class saw Nicola's potential, but there was a problem: women's boxing was banned in England at the time. This didn't stop Nicola, and when the ban was lifted in 1996 she knew she wanted to win the Olympics. She didn't get to fight for four years because, even though the ban got lifted, there were no other girls for her to fight. She could spar against boys in training, but she wasn't allowed to box them in competitions.

There weren't many fights in Britain so Nicola had to travel abroad to find decent competition. There was no funding for this so she worked as a builder to pay for these trips. In 2001 she became the first female boxer to represent England. In 2007 she won a silver medal at the European Championships, followed by a silver at the World Championships. In 2009 Nicola heard the news she was desperate for: women's boxing was going to be in the London 2012 Olympics. Training began, but that year Nicola fell down some stairs, cracking a vertebra in her back. Her recovery was long and painful but Nicola slowly worked back to peak fitness, winning another silver at the World Championships. Two years later she made history by winning gold in front of her home crowd in London 2012.

Nicola continued winning, taking gold at the 2014 Commonwealth Games. In Rio 2016 she added another Olympic gold to her collection and then she turned to professional boxing. Nicola remained undefeated and won a WBO belt.

PAVE THE WAY *like a* GIRL
Manon Rhéaume

Full name: **Manon Rhéaume**
Sport: **Ice hockey**
Birth date: **February 24, 1972**
Place of birth: **Beauport, Quebec, Canada**
Team: **Canada**
Best achievements: **Silver Olympic medalist and first woman to play in the NHL**

Did you know...?

★ Manon played on the national women's team, winning gold at two World Championships. She also went to the Olympics in 1998. This was the first time women's ice hockey was included and she won a silver medal.

★ Manon is the only woman to have played in the top four major North American professional leagues.

★ When Manon retired from hockey in 2000 she joined Mission Hockey as director of global marketing, helping to design ice hockey products specifically for women.

When you become the first in the world to reach a major milestone there is nobody to show you the way. Ice hockey player Manon Rhéaume forged an awesome career in a sport that is traditionally dominated by men.

Manon's father built an ice rink in the back yard and this was where she learned to skate at three years old. When her brother's hockey team needed a goalie she stepped in. It's a position that requires a cool head and quick reactions, and Manon was good at it. Her teammates accepted her straight away, but others did not. The first time she tried out for the top-tier team she didn't get picked. She was playing well and couldn't understand why she was passed over for players who weren't as good as her. The coaches told her parents it was because she was a girl. This made Manon more determined to win, and eventually a coach gave her a shot, impressed with her skill.

Hockey pucks travel at 100 miles per hour (161km/h) and it was Manon's job to stop them. If she let on that she was hurt she'd be told that girls shouldn't be there, so she just kept playing. Her love for the game was the reason she persisted, but she never thought there would be a career in it—no girls had got into professional leagues.

Before Manon left for university she got a summer job at a TV station. Her first assignment was a National Hockey League (NHL) match. Here she met Tampa Bay Lightning manager Phil Esposito. He had seen footage of her playing and invited her to an NHL training camp.

She was very excited about this opportunity, but when she walked into the training room the guys were so big and she felt so small. On the ice however she held her own, blocking shot after shot, and Esposito decided to play her in a preseason exhibition match.

Just before the match Manon felt nervous. She found a bouquet of flowers in the locker room addressed to her. They were from a radio station in Montreal with a message that said: "You are not alone. We are all behind you." These words gave her confidence and as soon as she got onto the ice her head was in the game, her nerves gone. Manon saved seven out of nine shots in a performance that earned her a pro contract in the minor leagues.

DANCE *like a* GIRL
Misty Copeland

Full name: **Misty Danielle Copeland**
Sport: **Ballet**
Birth date: **September 10, 1982**
Place of birth: **Kansas City, Missouri, USA**
Team: **American Ballet Theatre**
Best achievement: **Principal dancer for the American Ballet Theatre**

Did you know...?

★ Misty made history when she became the first African American female principal dancer for the American Ballet Theatre.

★ In 2009 Misty worked with singer Prince, starring in his *Crimson and Clover* music video and joining him on tour.

★ Misty went through a tough legal battle between her mother and her coach Cindy. Her mother wanted her back home, Cindy wanted her to continue her studies, and Misty was caught between the two. In the end Misty's mother promised that she could continue her lessons.

"YOU CAN START LATE, LOOK DIFFERENT, BE UNCERTAIN AND STILL SUCCEED."

Misty Copeland is one of the biggest names in ballet, taking the lead role in some of the world's grandest performances. This is something she has had to fight for every step of the way, shattering barriers and carving her own path to success.

Misty didn't come from a place of privilege, nor did she start dancing at an early age. Instead she came from a very unstable home environment where her family moved around a lot. At the age of 13 she was sleeping on the floor in a motel room with her five brothers and sisters. Her mother had to work long hours to scratch together enough money to feed them all. Misty was shy as a child, but one of her school teachers saw talent in her and encouraged her to attend ballet classes. It was here that she met ballet teacher Cindy Bradley.

Cindy was so impressed with Misty that she offered her a scholarship. In three months Misty was dancing en pointe (on her tiptoes). This skill normally takes ballerinas years to perfect. But the two-hour bus ride to get to training each day was difficult and her mother told Misty to quit. Cindy didn't want Misty's talent going to waste and offered to let Misty stay with her during the week so she could continue her ballet studies, and her mother agreed.

Misty was dancing professionally within a year and won an LA Music Center Spotlight Award. Her rapid rise to success was unprecedented in classical dancing.

The opportunity with the American Ballet Theatre came when she was invited to a summer program in New York. She made a good impression and was invited to join the company full time, and Misty accepted the offer once she had finished school. She progressed quickly, becoming one of the youngest soloists in the ABT. She took leading roles in The Firebird and Swan Lake among many other notable productions. In 2015 Misty was promoted to principal dancer, continuing to deliver outstanding performances.

As well as the growing number of accolades, Misty has also received some harsh criticism throughout her career. She was frequently told that she had the wrong body to be a ballet dancer. It wasn't easy, but Misty has changed the idea of what a perfect dancer should look like.

CLIMB MOUNTAINS *like a* GIRL
Arunima Sinha

From a hospital bed to standing on the top of the world, Arunima Sinha's story radiates willpower, persistence, and mental toughness. She is chasing her goal around the globe, with a mission to climb the highest mountain on each continent.

On April 12, 2011 Arunima caught the train to Delhi. She had applied for a job as head constable with the armed forces and was traveling to the capital city to sort out a mistake on her paperwork. Sitting quietly on the train, she was attacked by robbers who tried to snatch her gold necklace. When she fought back they threw her off the train. Arunima tried to get up off the ground, but before she could move another train ran over her leg.

Arunima was found by villagers the next morning and eventually taken to hospital. To save her life, doctors had to amputate her leg.

While she was recovering she decided she was going to climb Mount Everest. This was the toughest challenge she could think of and she wanted to prove to everybody around her, as well as herself, that she could do it. People didn't believe in her dream, but this only made Arunima more determined.

To begin with Arunima could hardly walk, but she trained under Bachendri Pal (the first Indian woman to successfully scale Mount Everest) and worked her way up to bigger and bigger mountains. On May 21, 2013 Arunima reached the summit

"SET YOUR GOALS HIGH AND DON'T STOP UNTIL YOU REACH THEM."

Full name: **Arunima Sinha**
Sport: **Mountaineering**
Birth date: **July 20, 1989**
Place of birth: **Ambedkar Nagar, India**
Best achievement: **Climbed the highest peaks in six of the seven continents (so far!)**

of Mount Everest. It took her 52 days to make the grueling climb, pushing on even when her Sherpa suggested she turn back. She was running low on oxygen and might not have enough for the return journey. Everest was her dream and she was going to achieve it, so she kept going, making it to the top and safely back down again. In doing so, Arunima became the first female amputee to climb Everest. Arunima has gone on to conquer the highest peak in six of the seven continents so far. This includes Kilimanjaro (Africa), Elbrus (Europe), Kosciuszko (Australia), Aconcagua (South America), and Vinson (Antarctica).

Did you know...?

★ Before the attack on the train Arunima was a very good volleyball player, competing at national level.

★ Arunima runs a non-profit sports academy for disabled children, giving them opportunities to help them realize their potential.

★ Arunima is also the first female amputee in the world to climb Mount Vinson, which is the highest peak in Antarctica.

COACH *like a* GIRL
Tracey Neville

Full name: **Tracey Anne Neville MBE**
Sport: **Netball**
Birth date: **January 21, 1977**
Place of birth: **Bury, Manchester, UK**
Team: **England**
Best achievements: **Commonwealth Games bronze medalist and award-winning coach**

Did you know...?

★ Tracey started playing on an adult team at the age of nine. Her mother played in the local league and Tracey joined in. After proving her worth as a goal shooter she became a permanent fixture.

★ Tracey has a degree in nutrition and worked as a strength and conditioning coach, both of which have made her a better player and a better coach.

★ Netball is not an Olympic sport which means that funding is tight. When Tracey was playing she had to balance a part-time job around her training and competitions.

"I DON'T PREPARE MY TEAM FOR THE FAIL."

If you consistently turn up on time and give maximum effort, then nobody can ask for more. This was the advice given to Tracey Neville by her parents. It proved to be a winning formula in the Neville family. Her mother was the general manager of Bury Football Club, her father was a professional cricketer, and her brothers were both pretty good at soccer.

Netball was Tracey's sport and by 14 she'd made it on to the county team. International success came in the form of a bronze medal at the Commonwealth Games in Kuala Lumpur 1998. This was the first major netball medal for team England. Tracey managed an impressive 81 caps over 15 years, but by the age of 27 she'd had five knee operations and by 30 she was forced to retire. Success in sport isn't just about playing though. Athletes need a really strong team around them.

Tracey moved into coaching, applying the same competitive mentality to leading a team as she did playing for one. Her first position was with Northumbria, a struggling team at the bottom of the league. Turning things around was difficult, but she worked hard. Her efforts didn't go unnoticed and she was soon headhunted by Manchester Thunder, coaching them to two Superleague titles.

In 2015 a big opportunity came her way: head coach for England. Tracey leapt at this chance and created a team that worked well together, rather than prioritizing individual talent. She demanded a lot from her players: commitment, hard work, and team work. Her results did the talking as the Roses started to rise up the rankings.

At the 2018 Commonwealth Games, the Roses pulled out a sensational comeback to beat Jamaica in the semi-finals. Next up they faced Australia, the world number one team and favorites to win. This was the Roses' first ever major final. They worked well together, executed the game plan, and fought a close match. With the scores tied, a penalty shot in the last seconds put the Roses one point ahead, enough to clinch the gold. Tracey was with the team every step of the way, offering inspirational team talks, and finding where players could raise their game.

THROW *like a* GIRL
Dame Valerie Adams

Full name: **Dame Valerie Kasanita Adams**
Sport: **Shot put**
Birth date: **October 6, 1984**
Place of birth: **Rotorua, New Zealand**
Team: **New Zealand**
Best achievement: **Two Olympic gold medals**

Did you know...?

★ Valerie, the youngest New Zealand woman to become a dame, has won gold at the youth, junior, and senior World Championships.

★ Valerie struggled to get pregnant but IVF treatment enabled her to give birth to two children. She has spoken out about fertility issues and is also doing a great job of balancing motherhood with training.

A champion refuses to quit no matter how many challenges are thrown their way. Shot putter Valerie Adams has fought hard to achieve world domination, overcoming adversity to consistently come out on top.

When Valerie reluctantly tried shot put her teacher saw her potential and encouraged her to take part in school competitions. It took her less than a year to qualify for the Youth World Championships. Her biggest supporter was her mother and with the help of the local community they raised funds to get her there. But not long after that Valerie's mother found out she had terminal cancer. For three months 15-year-old Valerie didn't go to school while she nursed her mother. Watching the opening ceremony of the Sydney 2000 Olympic Games, Valerie was inspired to take her shot put to this level. The next morning her mother passed away.

Her stepfather remarried shortly afterwards and Valerie found herself without a home. She moved in with her coach Kirsten Hellier and the following year she won gold at the Youth World Championships. Her dream of competing at the Olympic Games became a reality in 2004 when she made the team for Athens. Things were looking good, but six weeks before the Games she was rushed to hospital to have her appendix out. Not ideal preparation, but Valerie still managed a very respectable seventh-place finish.

Valerie continued to seize titles at World Championships, even winning in 2007 with a torn ligament in her throwing hand. As reigning world champion, Valerie felt under pressure to deliver results in Beijing 2008. She took the lead from the start with a new personal best. She didn't need her last throw: she had already won.

In 2010 her coach stepped down and this decision hit Valerie hard. In London 2012 she threw 20.70m to earn gold. In Rio 2016 she performed well, but was edged out by Michelle Carter, and in Tokyo 2020 she took bronze, her fourth Olympic medal.

"ONCE YOU GET TO ANY HIGH PRESSURE SITUATION IT'S ALL A MENTAL GAME."

Maggie Alphonsi

Full name: **Margaret Alphonsi MBE**
Sport: **Rugby union**
Birth date: **December 20, 1983**
Place of birth: **Lewisham, London, UK**
Team: **England**
Best achievement: **2014 World Cup winner**

"YOU NEVER KNOW WHAT YOU CAN ACHIEVE UNTIL YOU PUSH YOURSELF."

Maggie's journey into rugby started in North London where she grew up with a talent for music and a passion for sport. School was another story. Maggie's behavior was poor and she often got into trouble. Her PE teacher Liza Burgess, captain of the Welsh rugby team, urged her to try rugby. She thought that the rugby pitch would be a great place for Maggie to run off her energy and attitude. Initially Maggie wasn't keen, but she went along to her local rugby club, Saracens, and started training.

As 16 she was picked to play in a tournament in Australia. The trip was self-funded, however, and way out of Maggie's budget. But her school was supportive, with teachers helping her to fundraise what she needed. When she realized her teachers were willing to help her, Maggie decided to quit messing around. She knuckled down in school and her grades improved, allowing her to go to university to study sport and exercise science.

At university Maggie's international career took off. She put on the England shirt for the senior team aged 19, quickly making a name for herself as a flanker. In 2006 she competed in her first World Cup, where England reached the final but the team from New Zealand proved too formidable. Maggie channeled the loss, using it to spur her on to better performances in the future. England were proving to be a dominant force in the Six Nations, but that World Cup title was elusive. In 2010 they were beaten on home soil in the finals by New Zealand again. An injury took Maggie out of play for 20 months but she returned in November 2013, just in time for her third World Cup. England beat Canada to take home the title for the first time in 20 years.

Did you know...?

- Maggie was a pundit for the 2015 Rugby World Cup, making her the first former female player to commentate on a men's international game.

- Maggie was born with a club foot. While she was never going to be the quickest, she worked hard to maximize her strengths.

- She was the first woman given the Pat Marshall Award, which is awarded to outstanding rugby personalities.

RACE *like a* GIRL
Jasmin Paris

Full name: **Jasmin Karina Paris**
Sport: **Fell running**
Birth date: **November 19, 1983**
Place of birth: **Manchester, UK**
Best achievement: **Winner and world record holder of the Spine Race**

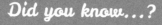

Did you know...?

- Many athletes focus on their sport like a full-time job, but not Jasmin. She works as a vet and to fit in her training she gets up at 5am to run before work.

- She is also currently working towards a PhD at the University of Edinburgh, trying to find a cure for a type of cancer called acute myeloid leukaemia.

- Jasmin continued to train when she was pregnant with her daughter. She even managed a fell race ten days before she gave birth and was back in training four weeks after her baby was born.

"DO SOMETHING YOU LOVE AND BELIEVE IN YOURSELF ENOUGH TO GIVE IT A GO."

Surrounded by beautiful landscapes and exposed to all weather conditions, fell running is just as much about mental stamina as it is physical endurance. Ultra-distance runner Jasmin Paris is very good at what she does, delivering exceptional results on challenging terrain.

Jasmin grew up surrounded by hills and loves being outdoors, but she didn't start fell running until she finished university. One of her colleagues told her about a local fell race and she decided to sign up for it. While she didn't place in the top half she enjoyed every muddy step. For Jasmin, it is the love of the mountains, the stunning scenery, and the sense of freedom that comes from running on the fells that inspires her to tackle some of the world's most demanding races. She found a talent for the longer ultra-distance races and it didn't take long before she was making a name for herself.

When Jasmin breaks records, she doesn't shave off a couple of seconds from the previous time, she obliterates them. She took two and a half hours off the Bob Graham record, a grueling 66 miles (106km) over 42 summits in the Lake District. She broke the men's record for the Ramsey Round by 46 minutes, a notoriously brutal challenge over 24 Scottish summits. And she smashed the record for

the Paddy Buckley round in Wales. She extended the women's record for the 61-mile (98km), 47-peak race in Snowdonia by 29 minutes. The same year she completed these three events she was awarded the Extreme Skyrunning World Title after winning the Tromsø SkyRace and the Glen Coe Skyline.

In 2019 Jasmin achieved something spectacular. She won the Spine Race, beating all 136 male and female competitors to the finish line. The Spine is classed as the UK's toughest fell race. It's 268 miles (431km) long and it's held in the middle of winter across rugged terrain. In previous years over half the competitors haven't reached the finish line.

Jasmin completed it in 83 hours, 12 minutes, and 23 seconds. This was another record-breaking time, where she smashed the men's record by more than 12 hours. What makes this even more exceptional is that she stopped on route to pump breast milk for her baby daughter.

SKI *like a* GIRL
Menna Fitzpatrick

Nobody achieves success on their own. Reaching goals is a team effort, and alpine skier Menna Fitzpatrick shows just how much you can achieve when people work together.

Menna was born blind in her left eye and with 5% vision in her right, but her parents were determined she'd have the same opportunities as her sisters. She learned to ski when she was five, and that's when she decided she wanted to go to the Paralympics. A goal that big requires a lot of practice, so she made regular trips to an indoor slope and by 2010 she had an invitation to train with the national squad.

Weaving around poles and hurtling downhill at speeds up to 70 miles per hour (113km/h), the aim of skiing is to get to the bottom of the course as fast as possible. But how do you do this when you can't see? Visually impaired athletes work with a sighted guide, who skis just ahead of them. The guide wears a bright jacket and a headset, giving instructions as they descend. The skier needs to know which direction to go, how steep the slope is, the condition of the snow, and how fast to ski. A skier places all their faith in their guide because any errors can be catastrophic.

Menna teamed up with Major Jen Kehoe in 2015, and they made a formidable team. Jen serves in the army, who allowed her to train full time, and the pair developed a strong relationship that delivered awesome results. They were strong medal contenders, but in 2016 Menna broke her hand while training and had to take two months off. Despite this, they won a bronze medal at the World Championships, but they knew they could do better.

A year later they proved this at the PyeongChang 2018 Winter Paralympic Games. Although Menna crashed out of the downhill, she used that to motivate herself and they won a bronze medal in the super-G, followed by two silvers in the combined and giant slalom. Menna and Jen gave it their all on the slalom, winning gold on their last run.

After Jen retired, Menna teamed up with Katie Guest and at Beijing 2022 they won silver in the super-G and bronze in the combined.

★ Paralympic guides also receive medals. Jen stood beside Menna on the podium, and rightly so! She worked just as hard as Menna. Both were awarded MBEs after their PyeongChang performance.

★ After winning the gold medal in PyeongChang, Menna and Jen celebrated by having a cup of tea.

★ With six Paralympic medals, Menna is Britain's most decorated Winter Paralympian.

Full name: **Menna Fitzpatrick MBE**
Sport: **Alpine skiing**
Birth date: **May 5, 1998**
Place of birth: **Macclesfield, Cheshire, UK**
Team: **Great Britain**
Best achievement: **Paralympic gold medalist**

"BE BRAVE EVERY DAY AND PUSH YOURSELF TO THE LIMIT."

SCORE *like a* GIRL
Marta

In team sports it is often difficult for one player to shine, but Marta Vieira da Silva—known worldwide simply as Marta—is an exception to the rule. Regarded as one of the best soccer players in the world, she is admired for her unparalleled ability on the pitch and her determination to excel.

Marta comes from one of Brazil's poorest regions. Her father left when she was a baby, so Marta's mother worked long hours. Her older brother José introduced her to soccer and they played barefoot in the streets. Every day people told her that soccer wasn't a girls' sport and that she wasn't going to make it. Even her family doubted her ambitions. But Marta had a dream of making it to the top and this was far greater than any criticism. Her talent got her on the boys' team, but even then she wasn't fully accepted. She still received hurtful comments, she was still treated differently, and she was pulled from tournaments for no other reason than she was a girl.

Marta's tenacity paid off. At 14 she took a three-day bus ride to Rio de Janeiro where the coach signed her as soon as she saw her play. The women's national league was newly formed in Brazil and the money wasn't great. She sent what little she earned back to her family, but faced a big setback when her team was cut a year later. She kept playing and people started to take notice. Three years later Marta received a phone call that changed her life. She got a transfer to Umeå IK in Sweden, where women's soccer was much more established. She stayed there for six years, proving to be a top scorer and helping her team win three league titles and a UEFA Cup. Everybody wanted the best player in the world and Marta played in the USA, Brazil, and Sweden, before finally settling with Orlando Pride, where she has been voted Most Valuable Player.

On the international scene, Marta won silver in Athens 2004 and Beijing 2008, and carried the Olympic flag in her home games in Rio 2016. She is best known for her goal scoring. In fact, her record of a whopping 17 goals at World Cup tournaments is unbeaten, and she's the first soccer player ever to score at five different World Cups and five consecutive Olympic Games.

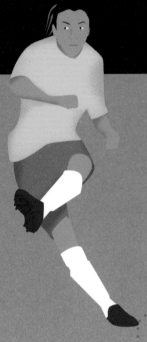

"BELIEVE IN YOURSELF AND TRUST YOURSELF."

Did you know...?

★ Marta is a UN Goodwill Ambassador for girls and women in sport. She wants to inspire girls to challenge stereotypes and achieve their ambitions.

★ Marta has been named FIFA World Player of the Year six times, winning from 2006 to 2010 and again in 2018. No other soccer player has this many wins.

★ An imprint of Marta's feet was set in cement outside the Estádio do Maracanã in Rio. She was the first woman to be awarded this honor. In Brazil it was illegal for women to play soccer until 1979.

Full name: **Marta Vieira da Silva**
Sport: **Soccer**
Birth date: **February 19, 1986**
Place of birth: **Dois Riachos, Alagoas, Brazil**
Teams: **Orlando Pride and Brazil**
Best achievement: **Two Olympic silver medals**

DARE TO DREAM *like a* GIRL
Yusra Mardini

Full name: **Yusra Mardini**
Sport: **Swimming**
Birth date: **March 5, 1998**
Place of birth: **Damascus, Syria**
Team: **Refugee Olympic Team**
Best achievement: **Competed at the Rio 2016 and Tokyo 2020 Olympic Games**

Did you know...?

★ Yusra wants to change how people see refugees. She wants to encourage people to give refugees a chance to achieve their dreams.

★ She is the youngest ever Goodwill Ambassador for the United Nations' refugee agency. In this role Yusra has spoken to world leaders and advocates for refugees.

★ Yusra and Sara's mother, father, and sister Shahed were granted asylum months after them.

Yusra Mardini stood under the Olympic rings in Rio 2016 and Tokyo 2020 instead of her national flag. She risked death to leave her war-torn country and refused to let her sporting dream die on the way.

Yusra grew up in Damascus where her father taught her how to swim. Yusra didn't really enjoy the sport, but watching the 2004 Olympics on TV filled her with a burning ambition to become a champion. Yusra's training increased and her results improved. By 12 she had made it onto the Syrian national team. At the World Junior Championships she broke the Syrian record for 400m freestyle.

War in Syria broke out when Yusra was 13. With bombs falling and tanks rolling through the streets, swimming stopped being important and life was about survival. Yusra fled Syria with her older sister Sara and started the perilous journey to Germany. With 18 other refugees, they crowded onto a small dinghy to cross the sea to Greece. After just 15 minutes the engines died. The sea was choppy and, with too many people on board, the boat was in danger of capsizing. Yusra jumped into the water with Sara and two others and grabbed a rope. For over three hours they treaded water until they made it safely to shore.

To get to Germany Yusra and Sara slept rough, paid smugglers to transport them across Europe, and sneaked across borders. They got hungry and cold, and spent a night in a Hungarian prison, and they were refused entry to many hotels and restaurants. It took 25 days to reach Germany where they received a warm welcome. Strangers offered kindness, and when Yusra spoke of her swimming ambitions she was invited to practice at a local pool. Yusra restarted her intensive training regime.

How do you go to the Olympics when you no longer have a country? In recognition of the millions of people around the world without a home, the IOC created the Refugee Olympic Team. Ten athletes represented refugees around the world in Rio 2016, and Yusra fulfilled her dream of competing at the Olympics. At Tokyo 2020, she carried the team's flag at the opening ceremony. Yusra is continuing her training, as well as her work as an activist to give refugees a voice.

"I WANT EVERYONE NOT TO GIVE UP ON THEIR DREAMS. EVEN IF IT'S IMPOSSIBLE, YOU NEVER KNOW WHAT WILL HAPPEN."

CYCLE *like a* GIRL
Dame Laura Kenny

Cyclist Laura Kenny has an impressive trophy cabinet. On the track she demonstrates an ultra-competitive streak and razor-sharp focus, which has seen her rise to become one of the most successful Olympic athletes of all time.

Laura was born a month too early. She spent the first six weeks of her life in intensive care and was later diagnosed with asthma. Doctors recommended that she do plenty of exercise to help improve her breathing. She joined a local cycling club with her family and they were hooked. Laura was soon racing, winning the National Championships at 12 and getting an invitation to the Olympic Development Program at 15.

Laura competes in the women's team pursuit, the omnium, and the madison. These are very different disciplines, but Laura excels at them all. For the team pursuit three riders race over 3km. The winner of the omnium is the athlete who performs best over four different events. In the madison teams of two race over 120 laps, scoring points in sprints every ten laps and for lapping their rivals.

In London 2012 Laura won gold in the team pursuit with teammates Dani King and Joanna Rowsell, breaking the world record. Two days later she won gold in the omnium. She peddled furiously fast, pushing through the pain in her legs to deliver the goods in a nail-biting final.

Winning in London turned Laura into a household name, but it also upped the pressure she felt she was under. Laura gets nervous as she waits for the race to begin. Negative thoughts pop into her head. What if I can't do this? This is a natural response. She desperately wants to win. With the support of her coaches and sport psychology techniques, Laura has learned how to channel nerves into a positive energy. When she gets out there on the bike, her focus is on the race and her nerves disappear. Heading into Rio 2016 Laura was the favorite to win. She overcame heavy expectations to come away with two gold medals, and followed this up with a fifth gold and a silver in Tokyo 2020.

"YOU DON'T KNOW HOW GOOD YOU ARE UNTIL YOU ACTUALLY GET OUT ON A BIKE AND GET RIDING."

Did you know...?

With five gold medals, Laura is Great Britain's most successful female athlete in any sport.

Laura married fellow cyclist Jason Kenny shortly after the Rio Olympics. Their baby Albie was born in 2017. After a short break she got back on the bike and resumed her training, winning silver medals in the 2018 and 2019 World Championships.

Laura has 15 World Championship medals, ten European Championship medals, and a Commonwealth gold.

Full name: **Dame Laura Rebecca Kenny DBE**
Sport: **Cycling**
Birth date: **April 24, 1992**
Place of birth: **Harlow, Essex, UK**
Team: **Great Britain**
Best achievement: **Five Olympic gold medals**

JUMP *like a* GIRL
Mariya Lasitskene

When the World Anti Doping Association banned Russia from all majo sporting events athletes who had never taken performance-enhancing drugs were excluded as well as those that had. But high jumper Mariya Lasitskene wasn't going to give up on her Olympic dreams.

Some athletes don't play by the rules. Rather than letting their hard work and natural abilities do the talking, they take substances that allow them to recover quicker, focus better, or build bigger muscles. This is not allowed, and any athlete who gets caught will be stripped of their medals and banned from future competitions. It is bad enough when a single athlete cheats, but it is far worse when the national team gets behind it. Russia got caught repeatedly abusing the system. Coaches pressured athletes to take pills and officials switched tainted urine samples with clean ones. In 2015, Russia was banned from competing in world track and field events until they cleaned up their act.

But what happens if you're a Russian athlete who doesn't take performance-enhancing substances? High jumper Mariya Lasitskene faced this problem when she was banned from the Olympic Games in Rio

2016. Mariya had shot onto the high-jump scene with a silver medal at the 2009 World Youth Championships. She later took gold at the Youth Olympics with a jump of 1.89m. Many juniors find the leap to senior level tough, but not Mariya. She came joint first at her first senior World Championships in 2014, jumping a magnificent 2.0m. All this made her the favorite to win the gold medal at Rio, but her Olympic dream was over for now because of the actions of the state.

Not getting to go to the Olympics in 2016 hurt, and she was determined to overcome the barriers holding her back. Before the 2017 World Championships she applied for status as a neutral athlete, and because of her clean record it was granted. She didn't compete under her national flag in Tokyo 2020, but under her own esteem. Here, she achieved her dream of competing at the Olympics and jumped her way to the gold medal.

Full name: **Mariya Aleksandrovna Lasitskene**
Sport: **High jump**
Birth date: **January 14, 1993**
Place of birth: **Prokhladny, Russia**
Team: **Neutral**
Best achievement: **Olympic gold medalist and five-time world champion**

Did you know...?

★ Mariya has been very vocal about doping reforms in Russia. She is calling for coaches and officials implicated in the doping scandal to quit and let a new generation of athletes be led by better principles.

★ Mariya won 45 competitions in a row over a two-year period from July 2016 to July 2018.

★ Mariya's current coach was her school teacher. He recognized her talents for high jump when she was seven years old, and continues to support her through her career.

"IT IS AN AWFUL SITUATION, BUT IT IS IN OUR POWER TO CHANGE IT."

INSPIRE *like a*
Sarah Williams

Full name: **Sarah Williams**
Sport: **Adventuring**
Place of birth: **Wirral, Merseyside, UK**
Best achievement: **Influential contemporary adventurer**

Did you know...?

★ Sarah's award-winning *Tough Girl* podcast has over two million downloads, showcasing female sporting talent from around the world.

★ Before setting up Tough Girl Challenges Sarah ran the London Marathon five times, climbed a live volcano in Chile, and cycled Death Road in Bolivia. With steep drops and tight bends, this is the most dangerous road in the world.

★ Sarah has a master's degree in women and gender studies. She went back to study while starting her business because she wanted a better understanding of the topic.

Tough girl. This sums up adventurer Sarah Williams beautifully. She's a fierce go-getter and challenge seeker. By pushing the boundaries of her own potential, she is also encouraging others to do the same.

Sarah has a mission. She inspires girls to step out of their comfort zones and try new things. After a high-flying career in finance she stepped away from the corporate world to set up her own business, Tough Girl Challenges, in 2014. This showcases female explorers, athletes, and adventurers, giving them a platform to share their stories and motivate others. The women she spoke to were pushing their bodies to the limit and achieving awesome things, so Sarah decided she ought to set a challenge of her own.

First up was the 2016 Marathon des Sables. This is called the toughest foot race on Earth for good reason. Sarah ran six marathons in six days through the Sahara Desert. The heat was blistering, water was rationed, and she had to carry everything she needed in a rucksack. This was an enormous challenge to tackle and it terrified her when she signed up, but Sarah broke it down into more manageable stages and focused on making it to the next checkpoint, then the next, and the next.

Sarah's next adventure was the Appalachian Trail. This is the longest hiking trail in the world, stretching 2,190 miles (3,524km) down the Appalachian mountain range on the east coast of America. It usually takes six months to walk, but a man had finished the trail in 100 days and Sarah thought if he could do it then so could she, and she did. It wasn't easy though. There were moments where Sarah worried whether she was going to make it in her time frame, and this is where she had to dig deep, manage her emotions, and find the motivation to keep going.

Sarah hasn't stopped there. In 2018 she cycled over 2,500 miles (4,023km) from Canada to Mexico. The following year she hiked the Camino Portugués, a 420-mile (676km) coastal walk from Lisbon to Spain, and it took her 23 days to walk the 315-mile (507km) Lycian Way in southern Turkey. In 2022 she completed the 870-mile (1400km) Wales Coastal Path in 50 days. Along the way Sarah continues to inspire girls to start their own challenges.

"IF IT DOESN'T CHALLENGE YOU, IT DOESN'T CHANGE YOU."

SWING *like a* GIRL
Shanshan Feng

Full name: **Shanshan Feng**
Sport: **Golf**
Birth date: **August 5, 1989**
Place of birth: **Guangzhou, China**
Team: **China**
Best achievements: **Winner of the LPGA Championships and Olympic bronze medalist**

Did you know...?

★ Shanshan opened her own junior golf academy in Guangzhou so young people have access to coaches and facilities.

★ Shanshan likes to wear black-and-white cow-print clothes at tournaments. She wants to be remembered for enjoying every minute of her golf career, and her clothing reflects her personality.

★ When Shanshan moved to the US she couldn't speak much English. It was difficult to adjust, but Shanshan worked hard and quickly developed her independence.

In the golfing world Shanshan Feng displays awesome ability, and an even better attitude. She always tries her best at competitions, staying in the moment and taking it one shot at a time. If she doesn't win she learns how to get better for next time.

Shanshan started golf when she was ten years old. Golf was not very popular in China at the time. It had been banned by the Chinese government until the 1980s because it was seen as a game for the rich, and therefore against the Communist Party policy. As there weren't many facilities or coaches, Shanshan's father taught her to play. Every day Shanshan would go to school from eight in the morning until five in the evening, then she would hit balls at the driving range for two hours. At the weekend she would travel out of the city to play a round.

Shanshan started to win golf tournaments across China and people began to pay attention. Her talents were spotted by coach Gary Gilchrist. Impressed by her abilities he gave Shanshan a scholarship to his junior golf academy. There were very few opportunities for Shanshan to progress further in China, so at 17 she left her home and family behind and moved to the US. Her parents couldn't afford to come with her and they spent all their

savings to help Shanshan become the best golfer she could be.

Six months later Shanshan decided to try for the Ladies Professional Golf Association (LPGA). It's notoriously difficult to get a place on the LPGA Tour. Only the most talented female golfers in the world are invited to their events. Many people didn't believe Shanshan could do it. Nobody from China had made it as a professional golfer before, and she hadn't been training in the US for long. Shanshan proved them wrong, qualifying on her first attempt.

Shanshan has enjoyed a spectacularly successful career. She has won ten LPGA titles, becoming the first player from China to win a major golfing championship. She earned a number one world ranking, holding the position for 23 weeks. Shanshan also won the bronze medal at the Olympic Games in Rio. Golf had not been in the Olympics for 112 years. Shanshan hopes that her medal will encourage more people in China to take up the sport.

"ENJOY EVERY MINUTE OF IT."

ROW *like a* GIRL
Heather Stanning

Full name: **Major Heather Mary Stanning OBE**
Sport: **Rowing**
Birth date: **January 26, 1985**
Place of birth: **Yeovil, Somerset, UK**
Team: **Great Britain**
Best achievement: **Two Olympic gold medals**

Did you know...?

★ In London 2012, Heather and her rowing mate Helen won Great Britain's first gold medal of the Games. The pair also go down in history as the first ever female gold medalists rowing for Team GB.

★ Heather competes in the coxless pairs. This boat has two rowers, each with one oar. The boat doesn't have a person called a cox to steer the boat, so they have to make sure they stay on course while they row.

★ While she was training, Heather also managed to squeeze in time to do her army exams and was promoted to the rank of Major.

"I DON'T WANT TO FORGET WHAT IT IS LIKE TO LOSE, BECAUSE IF YOU LOSE SIGHT OF THAT YOU START TO THINK YOU ARE INVINCIBLE, AND THAT IS WHEN YOU COME UNSTUCK."

Success does not happen without hard work. This is something that rower Heather Stanning knows well. She is a formidable competitor, driven to give her all in the pursuit of excellence.

Every athlete has a different story about how they started their sport. Some elite athletes get into their chosen discipline at school, but Heather didn't start rowing until she was 20. She tried it at university as a way to make friends. Heather was invited to join the Start program, which trains talented beginners to GB squad level. Two years later she won the Under 23 World Championships, rowing in the coxless pairs with Olivia Whitlam.

Shortly after, Heather joined the British army. This was her dream for as long as she could remember and, after passing her training, she started as a Troop Commander in the Royal Artillery. She continued to row with the army, but her international career had taken a backseat. All that changed when she watched Olivia competing in the Beijing 2008 Olympic Games. It made Heather realize that she had more to give her sport. It could have been her out there, representing her country on the world's biggest stage.

The army were extremely supportive of Heather's Olympic bid and they allowed her to train full time. In 2010 she paired with Helen Glover. Their first World Cup saw a 9th-place finish, but with help from their coach they found their winning formula. They improved quickly, winning the silver medal at the World Championships later that year. From there Heather and Helen dominated the waters, soaring to a convincing victory in London 2012.

How do you celebrate an Olympic win? Heather went back to work. Six months later she was deployed to Afghanistan, completing a tour of duty in Helmand Province. When she returned to the UK her training for Rio resumed. Heather's place on the team wasn't guaranteed. She had to earn it. She had to get back to peak fitness and prove she was still capable of delivering results, and her efforts paid off. Once more Heather and Helen dominated the scene, flying across the water to win another gold in Rio 2016.

CLIMB *like a* GIRL
Sasha DiGiulian

Full name: **Sasha DiGiulian**
Sport: **Rock climbing**
Birth date: **October 23, 1992**
Place of birth: **Alexandria, Virginia, USA**
Best achievements: **Eight first ascents and over 30 first female ascents around the world**

Did you know...?

★ Sasha studied nonfiction writing and business at Columbia University, balancing her education with her training. Since graduating she has written articles for *National Geographic* and has a column in *Outside* magazine.

★ Noticing that there wasn't a rock-climbing emoji, Sasha contacted designers and submitted a proposal. If you search for the female climber emoji you'll see that it looks a bit like Sasha.

★ Her sport has taken a toll on her body and Sasha had both her hips reconstructed in 2021. She was told that she might never be able to climb again, but she's back training and is building up to bigger and bigger climbs.

Clinging by her fingertips hundreds of feet above the ground, Sasha DiGiulian is fast, fearless, and a force to be reckoned with. She epitomizes power and grace as she swings her body across the rock face and scales routes that haven't been conquered before.

Sasha's brother had a birthday party at the local rock climbing center and she loved it. She began climbing every week, and when she won her first competition against much older girls Sasha realized it could become more than a hobby. She started to spend more time climbing, squeezing it in around her school work. She won the Pan-American Championships at 11, and held on to this title for the rest of her junior career. Sasha took a gap year before university to focus on climbing, winning a gold, silver, and bronze medal at the senior World Championships. After this she moved away from competition climbing to outdoor projects.

Climbing routes are given different grades based on how difficult they are. At the age of 19 Sasha became the third woman to climb a 5.14d (9a), which is one of the hardest routes out there. Three years later she became the first woman to free climb the imposing 5,900ft (1,800m) north face of the Eiger in the Swiss Alps. It took three days for Sasha and her partner to reach the top, sleeping on hanging hammocks that they carried with them. When you're that high up you can't think about failing or give into your fears. Sasha was way out of her comfort zone, but she stayed focused on the moment and calculated every foot and hand placement with systematic precision.

The Eiger isn't the only record that Sasha has broken. She has over 30 first female ascents under her belt, traveling the world to seek new adventures and test her physical limits. She's scaled the Pico Cão Grande, a 1,210ft (370m) rocky needle surrounded by jungle in Sao Tome, Africa. She was the second person to conquer Mora Mora in Madagascar and she's tried her hand at ice climbing in Colorado. Sasha lives for difficult climbs and likes trying new things. An important part of this is being open to failure and using it to learn and grow.

"THE FUTURE IS UNKNOWN SO FOCUS ON THE PRESENT."

BEAT THE ODDS *like a* GIRL
Novlene Williams-Mills

Full name: **Novlene Hilaire Williams-Mills**
Sport: **Athletics**
Birth date: **April 26, 1982**
Place of birth: **St Ann Parish, Jamaica**
Team: **Jamaica**
Best achievement: **Four-time Olympic medalist**

Did you know...?

★ Novlene told very few people about her cancer diagnosis. During her recovery she had to learn to listen to her body and ignore the comments from other people who expected her to be running faster.

★ Novlene was named team captain for the Jamaican athletics team in London 2012. She was chosen for this honor in recognition of her work ethic and leadership skills.

★ Novlene is an ambassador for breast cancer awareness, working with charities to help women be more aware of early signs and symptoms, and also to find the beauty in survivor scars.

Winning a medal is seen as the pinnacle of an athlete's career, but the journey is often far more important. 400m runner Novlene Williams-Mills found incredible inner strength when she had to fight for her life and managed to bounce back to the track in winning form.

When you're preparing for the biggest tournament of your life you don't want distractions. You need your head in the game, your focus uninterrupted. A month before heading out to the London 2012 Olympic Games Novlene received some bad news. She had breast cancer. A diagnosis like this is scary and it left Novlene reeling. She looked after her body. It had never let her down before, and this felt like the worst kind of betrayal.

Novlene was in the prime of her career. Her first major international medal came in Athens 2004, where she won bronze in the 4x400m relay. She followed this up with silver in Beijing 2008, and continued to succeed at World Championship level. Getting cancer was a different kind of battle and Novlene had to figure out how to fight it. She decided to go ahead and compete in London, keeping quiet about her diagnosis. Stepping onto the start line nobody could see the fears that were keeping her up at night. She didn't know if this was going to be her last race. Novlene put in a solid performance to win another Olympic silver with her relay team. That evening she flew home, ready for surgery three days later.

Novlene had a double mastectomy, where both her breasts were removed. Five months and three surgeries later Novlene was finally cancer free. Her body had gone through so much and getting back to training was hard. Her recovery was a second chance in life and she wasn't going to waste it. Six months after her last surgery she won the National Championships in Jamaica. She laid down on the track and cried. Novlene continued to enjoy a successful career, performing better than she had pre-cancer. In 2014 she won a gold and silver at the Commonwealth Games, became Diamond League Champion, and was ranked world number one. In 2015 she was on the winning World Championship relay team and in Rio 2016 she won a silver medal.

"I CAN'T SPEND TIME STRESSING ABOUT SOMETHING I DON'T HAVE, AND JUST EMBRACE WHAT I DO HAVE."

RIDE *like a* GIRL
Sophie Christiansen

Full name: **Sophie Margaret Christiansen CBE**
Sport: **Para equestrian**
Birth date: **November 14, 1987**
Place of birth: **Berkshire, UK**
Team: **Great Britain**
Best achievement: **Eight Paralympic gold medals**

Did you know...?

★ Sophie graduated from Royal Holloway, University of London, with a first-class master's degree in mathematics.

★ She balances her training with a career as a software developer, writing code in different software languages.

★ Sophie is an outspoken campaigner for better services for people with disabilities. She promotes accessibility and has brought the issue to politicians' attention.

There is one name that stands out in the Paralympic equestrian world: Sophie Christiansen. Her glittering career has seen her bring medals home from four different Games.

Born two months prematurely, Sophie survived many medical problems. She had a fit, got blood poisoning and jaundice, her lung collapsed, and she had a heart attack. Sophie was also diagnosed with cerebral palsy in all four limbs. This affects movement in her arms and legs, as well as her speech. But it does not affect her aspirations, work ethic, and relentless pursuit of excellence.

Horse riding came at the suggestion of her physiotherapist. Sophie started riding when she was six and loved it. She couldn't walk or run like other children, but on a horse she found her freedom. She excelled at dressage, where the rider must form a close partnership with the horse to execute a precise routine. Sophie decided to take this as far as she could.

Sophie's first Paralympic Games was Athens 2004. At 16 she was the youngest athlete on the GB team, and she won a bronze medal. This experience was life changing for Sophie. Going into Athens she was shy and struggled to make friends.

Now, with a bronze medal around her neck, she started to get a lot of attention. The more interviews she did the more her confidence grew and people really took notice of what she was saying.

From that moment on Sophie's career soared. In Beijing 2008 she added to her medal collection with two golds and a silver. On home soil in London 2012 she won three golds, and in Rio 2016 she repeated this stunning performance with another three golds. Results like these are the product of hard work and the drive for continual improvement.

Sophie is honest about the setbacks she has experienced. She has spoken about the "post-Games blues" she felt after winning in Beijing. She came close to retiring after Rio 2016. When you have achieved your dream it can be hard to figure out what comes next. Taking time away to understand what you want to achieve is important, and Sophie continues to choose horse riding and the pursuit of gold.

"I WORK HARD TO REMOVE BARRIERS FROM MY LIFE."

SUCCEED *like a* GIRL
Dame Jessica Ennis-Hill

Full name: **Dame Jessica Ennis-Hill DBE**
Sport: **Heptathlon**
Birth date: **January 28, 1986**
Place of birth: **Sheffield, Yorkshire, UK**
Team: **Great Britain**
Best achievements: **Olympic gold medalist and three-time world champion**

> "THE ONLY ONE WHO CAN TELL YOU 'YOU CAN'T WIN' IS YOU, AND YOU DON'T HAVE TO LISTEN."

Did you know...?

★ Jessica studied psychology at the University of Sheffield. She had scholarship offers from American universities, but the training environment she had in Sheffield was right for her.

★ Jessica broke the British record for the heptathlon, 100m hurdles, high jump, and indoor pentathlon.

★ Jessica is now an entrepreneur. She set up Jennis, a business that provides home fitness programs for pregnant, post pregnant, and busy people.

A lethal combination of talent, hard work, and unassailable willpower saw heptathlete Jessica Ennis-Hill overcome challenges to win Olympic gold. Her drive to succeed captured the hearts of a nation, and spurred her on to deliver results when it mattered the most.

Jessica tried athletics at summer camp when she was ten years old. She was quick and explosive and strong. She took up the heptathlon, a sport that requires athletes to run, jump, and throw in seven different events. It's made up of the 100m hurdles, high jump, shot put, 200m, long jump, javelin, and 800m. Shooting onto the international scene, Jessica climbed up the ranking and won bronze at the 2006 Commonwealth Games.

Things were looking great in the lead up to the Olympics in Beijing 2008. She was one of Britain's best hopes for a medal, but an injury forced her to pull out. With broken bones in her foot there were fears that this would end her career. Jessica thought her Olympic dream was over and she was devastated.

It took 12 months to fully recover. A year of agonizing hard work, but Jessica came back stronger than ever. The following year she returned and took the heptathlon gold at the World Championships in Berlin with a new personal best. From that moment she was unstoppable. World and European titles fell at her feet, earning her a reputation as the one to beat. In the lead up to London 2012 Jessica was the heroine of the British team. She wasn't just holding her hopes and dreams, but carried those of a nation upon her shoulders.

Seeing her face on posters and billboards was a constant reminder of the pressure she was under, making it difficult to switch off away from the training field. Jessica admits she got nervous before competing, but she used that energy to deliver another personal best and gold-winning performance.

In 2014 she gave birth to her first child, taking the season off and missing the Commonwealth Games. She was not ready to retire however, and saw the return from having her baby as the new challenge she needed. Working on seven different events with a newborn was hard, but with the help of an amazing coaching and physio team Jessica dedicated herself to being both a mother and an elite athlete. After 15 months she went on to win her third World Championship gold medal in Beijing, followed by silver at the 2016 Rio Olympic Games.

SKATE *like a* GIRL
Sky Brown

Full name: **Sky Brown**
Sport: **Skating**
Birth date: **July 12, 2008**
Place of birth: **Miyazaki, Japan**
Team: **Great Britain**
Best achievement: **Britain's youngest Olympic medal winner**

"YOU CAN DO ANYTHING NO MATTER WHAT AGE YOU ARE."

Sky Brown has rewritten the manual on what the world thinks young people are capable of. A skating superstar, she is brimming with passion, energy, and talent, and leaves everybody in awe as she holds her own against bigger and older athletes.

Sky can't remember a time when she hasn't skated. She started when she was three years old after watching her father performing tricks. Soon, the skateboard was her favorite toy and she'd spend all her spare time tearing it up at the skate park. It wasn't long before she was pulling off some impressive tricks. She'd fearlessly soar through the air and cruise up vertical ramps, and she loved going really fast. By seven she had attracted sponsorship deals, and at eight she became the youngest athlete to compete at the Vans US Open.

Sky is no stranger to falling. Scrapes and bruises are part of the learning process and she picks herself up and tries hard to nail the move next time. In 2020 she had a terrible crash in training, breaking her arm and fracturing her skull. She was told that she was lucky to be alive. In her hospital bed, she said "I'm excited to come back even stronger and even tougher. My heart wants to go so hard right now, I'm just waiting for my body to catch up."

This mindset has seen her compete against adults around the world. She won the UK Skateboarding Championships aged just ten,

a bronze medal at the 2019 World Championships a year later, and gold in the 2021 and 2022 X Games. And she had big ambitions to compete at the Olympics.

Sky's mother is Japanese and her father is British, so before the Tokyo 2020 Olympic Games she had a choice to make: which country should she represent? In the end she chose Great Britain because of the team's more relaxed approach. For Sky, skating is all about having fun. Whether she's practicing at the skate park or competing against the world's greatest, she just wants to try her best and enjoy herself. And it works! A few days after her thirteenth birthday, she won an Olympic bronze medal.

Did you know...?

★ Sky designed a skateboard and a percentage of the proceeds from sales go to a charity called Skateistan. They help children from poorer areas in the world access education and develop important skills.

★ When she's not skating, Sky likes to surf. She is good at it, too, and finds that it helps her with skating.

SWIM *like a* GIRL
Natalie du Toit

Full name: **Natalie du Toit MBE**
Sport: **Swimming**
Birth date: **January 29, 1984**
Place of birth: **Cape Town, South Africa**
Team: **South Africa**
Best achievements: **13 Paralympic gold medals and Olympian**

Did you know...?

★ In 2008 Natalie carried the South African flag in the Olympic and Paralympic opening ceremonies, making her the first to carry a flag in both events in the same year.

★ To raise money for charity, she swam over four and a half miles from Robben Island to Cape Town. Sharks are known to swim in these waters and it was colder than she was used to, but Natalie took it all in her stride. She was the first person back, beating the fastest man by just under a minute and broke the able-bodied women's world record.

★ Natalie has an impressive medal haul: 13 Paralympic golds, 12 World Championship golds, seven Commonwealth golds, and five All Africa Games golds. Can you imagine how big her trophy cabinet must be?

"EVEN WHEN BAD THINGS HAPPEN YOU HAVE TO TAKE THE POSITIVE OUT OF IT."

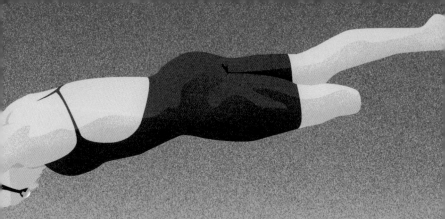

Swimmer Natalie du Toit had a dream. She wanted to represent her country at the Olympic Games, and was well on her way to achieving it. A sensation in the pool, she made the senior team for the 1998 Commonwealth Games at 14 years old. But three years later Natalie was knocked off her scooter after a swimming session and her left leg was amputated to save her life.

It wasn't long before Natalie was back in the pool where she learned to swim but with a missing limb. It was hard, but with her unfailing positive attitude Natalie was soon back up to standard. The following year she represented South Africa at the Commonwealth Games in Manchester, winning gold for the 50m and 100m freestyle races in the disability class and qualifying for the 800m in the able-bodied category. She was given the award for the Outstanding Athlete of the Games.

Switching to longer distances helped Natalie make up for slower starts and tumble turns. She narrowly missed out on qualifying for the Olympics in Athens 2004, but she did compete at the Paralympics where she dominated

her field with five golds, one silver, and four world records. Her Paralympic career blossomed.

At the 2008 able-bodied World Championships Natalie missed out on the podium by a fraction of a second. A valiant attempt, but a fourth-place finish in the 10k open water race secured her a spot in Beijing 2008. At the Olympics she finished 16th and was disappointed by her performance. She wanted to be in the top five. A few weeks later she swam in the Paralympic Games, adding another five gold medals to her collection. London 2012 was to be her last race. The build-up to the Games was tough for Natalie, but she gave it everything she could and came home with three gold medals and a silver.

FENCE *like a* GIRL
Valentina Vezzali

Fencer Valentina Vezzali has very few equals. Willpower and the desire to win have seen her rule her category unparalleled. What makes her even more exceptional is the career she built outside of sport, proving that it's possible to succeed in more than one area.

Six-year-old Valentina was taught how to fence by Ezio Triccoli. He was a legend in fencing circles. He learned the sport when he was in a prisoner of war camp during World War II. On his return to Italy he coached many athletes to Olympic success. Under his tutelage Valentina progressed quickly, winning her first national title four years later.

Valentina specializes in foil fencing. Success hinges on split-second decisions, quick reactions, and being able to anticipate your opponent's next move. This is something that Valentina excels at, and her lightning-fast strikes have earned her the nickname Cobra.

She made her Olympic debut in Atlanta 1996, returning home with a gold medal in the team event and silver as an individual. This kick-started a phenomenal career that spanned over 20 years. More golds followed in Sydney 2000, Athens 2004, Beijing 2008, and London 2012.

Valentina isn't just a talented fencer. She worked as a police officer where she reached the rank of superintendent. Valentina was also keen to have a family. In 2005 she gave birth to her first son, Pietro. Two and a half weeks later she was back in training. She built it up slowly, working hard to get back to competition fitness. Four months later she won gold at the World Championships in the individual category. She repeated this in 2013, taking another World Championship title three months after giving birth to her second son Andrea.

In 2013 she moved into politics. She wanted to give a voice to sport and was elected to the Italian Parliament Chamber of Deputies. Still competing, Valentina juggled her sports commitments with this new career and campaigned on women's rights, nutrition, sport, and physical education. She retired as fencer in 2016, after winning a silver medal at the World Championships in Rio.

Did you know...?

★ During her career, Valentina has won 16 World Championship gold medals, 11 World Cups, and 13 European golds.

★ Valentina's tremendous record sees her go down in history as the only fencer to win three individual gold medals in three consecutive Olympic Games.

★ Iesi, Valentina's hometown, produces very good fencers. In fact, an athlete from Iesi has been to every Olympic Games since 1976. What is remarkable about this is that Iesi is a relatively small town, with only 40,000 people.

Full name: **Maria Valentina Vezzali**
Sport: **Fencing**
Birth date: **February 14, 1974**
Place of birth: **Iesi, Italy**
Team: **Italy**
Best achievement: **Six-time Olympic gold medalist**

"I'M NOT AFRAID OF ANYONE, BECAUSE I'VE ALWAYS BELIEVED THAT YOUR OPPONENT, YOUR WORST OPPONENT, IS YOURSELF."

SAIL *like a* GIRL
Dame Ellen MacArthur

Full name: **Dame Ellen Patricia MacArthur DBE**
Sport: **Sailing**
Birth date: **July 8, 1976**
Place of birth: **Whatstandwell, Derbyshire, UK**
Best achievement: **Round-the-world record holder**

"WHEN I WAS OUT THERE I WAS NEVER EVER ALONE. THERE WAS ALWAYS A TEAM OF PEOPLE BEHIND ME, IN MIND IF NOT BODY."

Sometimes winning is about carrying on when others have given up long ago. It's about putting everything on the line and believing in your dreams. Ellen MacArthur shows that persistence can lead to greatness, pushing through barriers to pursue her love of sailing.

Ellen did not grow up near the sea. Instead she came from rural Derbyshire, which is as far from the sea as you can get in the UK. She was introduced to sailing by her aunt Thea. Ellen was hooked. She read everything there was to read on sailing and started to squirrel away her allowance. By 13 she had saved enough to buy a dinghy, which she named *Threp'ny Bit*. In between her school work Ellen took sailing courses, and when her exams were done she decided to give sailing a real shot. Her first expedition was sailing around Britain, which she completed at the age of 18.

To fund her ambitions Ellen lived on her boat and wrote thousands of letters, asking for sponsorship. Most of these went unanswered. Trying to get somebody else to believe in her idea was hard, but she didn't give up on her dream. Despite having little financial backing she sailed the Mini Transat from France to the Caribbean, finishing in 17th place.

Her determination eventually paid off. Kingfisher plc saw her potential and funded her to race the Route du Rhum from France to Guadeloupe. Ellen proved they'd made the right choice by winning.

The next goal Ellen set her heart on was the Vendée Globe, a solo race around the world, with no stops or help from others. She completed this journey in 94 days, returning home in second place. She was 24, the youngest competitor ever, and broke the record for the fastest woman.

Next Ellen wanted to be the fastest person to circumnavigate the globe single handed. She set out in November 2004. Ellen was tested by the elements and could only sleep for 20 minutes a time. After 71 days, 14 hours, and 18 minutes Ellen returned home, beating the record by a day.

Did you know…?

★ To earn a little extra cash, Ellen would carry out repair work and paint other people's yachts in the boatyard where she lived.

★ The Ellen MacArthur Foundation is a charity set up to help build a better future by keeping our stuff, from plastics to clothing, in use rather than becoming waste and pollution.

★ 20043 Ellenmacarthur is an asteroid named after her.

Kathrine Switzer

People can be quick to tell us that our dreams are too big. Sometimes this is out of thoughtlessness, sometimes out of spite, and sometimes because nobody ever attempted it before. One way to deal with people's negativity is to prove them wrong. Runner Kathrine Switzer did just that.

At college Kathrine joined the men's cross-country team because there weren't many sports clubs for women. She got the idea to run a marathon after her coach said he thought it was too far for a woman. This fired up Kathrine's determination and, on seeing this, her coach decided to help her. If she proved she could make the distance then he would take her to the Boston Marathon himself.

But it was 1967 and the Amateur Athletic Union (AAU) did not allow women to run more than 1.5 miles (2.4km) in competition. Once Kathrine had run 31 miles (50km) in training, her coach helped her register for the marathon. She entered as KV Switzer and her coach collected her race number for her. Two miles into the race the director spotted Kathrine, grabbed her, and tried to rip off her number. Kathrine was shaken up, but her boyfriend stepped in and blocked him. They ran on and Kathrine knew she had to cross the finish line. Four hours and 20 minutes later, she crossed the line. Her feet were so blistered they needed bandaging, but she had done it.

Kathrine tirelessly campaigned to change the AAU rules, and five years later women were officially allowed to run the Boston Marathon. Kathrine then organized a series of women-only distance races. Using data from these races she successfully lobbied to have the women's marathon included in the 1984 Olympics. Kathrine never gives up. Now over 75, she is still running and has created 261 Fearless, a non-profit organization that empowers women through running.

"ALL YOU NEED IS THE COURAGE TO BELIEVE IN YOURSELF, AND PUT ONE FOOT IN FRONT OF ANOTHER."

Did you know...?

★ Kathrine has run the Boston Marathon nine times, managing to complete the race in a time of two hours and 51 minutes. At the time this placed her as the sixth fastest marathon runner in the world.

★ Roberta Gibb was the first woman to run the Boston Marathon, doing it the year before Kathrine. She hid behind a bush at the start line and sneaked onto the course, but because she didn't officially enter the race her time was disqualified.

★ Fifty years after she first ran the Boston Marathon, Kathrine ran it again, at the age of 70. She was the first woman to run a marathon 50 years after her first marathon.

Full name: **Kathrine Virginia Switzer**
Sport: **Marathon running**
Birth date: **January 5, 1947**
Place of birth: **Amberg, Germany**
Best achievements: **First woman to officially run the Boston Marathon and led the drive to get the women's marathon included in the Olympic Games**

EXPLORE *like a* GIRL
Karen Darke

Full name: **Dr Karen Elisabeth Darke MBE**
Sports: **Adventuring, cycling, and triathlon**
Birth date: **June 25, 1971**
Place of birth: **Halifax, Yorkshire, UK**
Teams: **Great Britain and Scotland**
Best achievement: **Paralympic gold medalist**

"ABILITY IS A STATE OF MIND, NOT A STATE OF BODY."

Did you know...?

★ Karen researched gold content in rocks for a doctorate in geology. She returned to continue her PhD studies a year after her accident.

★ Karen also returned to rock climbing, famously scaling the 3,000ft (914m) El Capitan in Yosemite National Park, USA. She hauled herself up ropes attached to the cliff face with her arms, taking five days to make the climb.

★ One month after competing in London 2012 Karen went to a World Championships in a different sport, paratriathlon, where she won the gold medal.

For some athletes, sport is about pushing boundaries and redefining limits. Paralympian Karen Darke explores the depth of human adaptability and endurance, finding a way to live life on her terms and turn adversity into opportunity.

Karen was 21 when she had an accident. A rock-climbing trip turned into a disaster when she fell down a cliff. Waking up two days later she learned she was paralyzed and would never walk again. Life with a disability was a big adjustment, but Karen was determined that it wouldn't dampen her love for adventure and exploring. To find a way to reconnect with nature she had to focus on what she could do rather than what she couldn't, so she took up kayaking, hand-cycling, and adaptive skiing.

Karen's first major challenge was to cycle over 1,000 miles (1,609km) from Kyrgyzstan to Pakistan. Relying on the generosity of people they met on their way who shared their homes, food, and water, Karen and her friends reached their destination. This made her realize that she could achieve so much if she pushed herself out of her comfort zone. From there she hand-cycled the length of Japan and kayaked a thousand miles from Canada to Alaska.

Her next epic challenge was to cross Greenland's ice cap. Sitting on skis she propelled herself 372 miles (600km) with ski poles across the Arctic terrain. The wind got up to 200 miles per hour (320km/h), the temperature sat around –30°F (–34°C), and there had been sightings of polar bears. Hauling herself to heights of 6,500ft (1,980m) above sea level, Karen and her team spent 35 days making the crossing.

Although the sports Karen tried were more about pushing her own limits than being competitive, she started training with her handbike more seriously to try to compete at the Paralympics. In 2012 she won a silver medal in the road race at the London 2012 Paralympics. In her second race she crossed the finish line holding hands with teammate Rachel Morris. However, photos showed that Rachel's front wheel was fractionally ahead of Karen's and so she settled for fourth place.

In Rio 2016, Karen won Britain's 79th gold, and she decided to set out on another adventure: Quest 79. Karen's mission is to tackle nine long-distance bike rides on seven continents, finishing in Antarctica. At 79° south she wants to create a new pole, the Pole of Possibility. This epic journey isn't just to push herself, but about inspiring others to discover their limitless potential.

STAND OUT *like a* GIRL
Tamika Catchings

Full name: **Tamika Devonne Catchings**
Sport: **Basketball**
Birth date: **July 21, 1979**
Place of birth: **Stratford, New Jersey, USA**
Team: **USA**
Best achievement: **Four Olympic gold medals**

Did you know...?

★ Tamika studied sports management at the University of Tennessee and represented her university's team. Her coaches encouraged her to wear hearing aids again to help her become an even better player.

★ She is the first player to get a quintuple-double, where a player reaches double figures across five categories: points, blocked shots, assists, steals, and rebounds.

★ In 2004 Tamika set up the Catch The Stars Foundation. It helps young people achieve their potential, because without support it's difficult to shine.

Tamika Catchings spent many years trying to fit in, but ended up standing out as one of the greatest female basketball players of all time.

Tamika was born into a basketball family. Her father played in the National Basketball Association, and as a result they moved around a lot. When they settled in Texas, Tamika didn't fit in and the kids at her school let her know it. They singled her out and bullied her every day. Tamika had been born with moderate to severe hearing loss and had to wear chunky hearing aids. She hated feeling different to everyone else and, after a particularly brutal day at school, threw her hearing aids out. Her parents couldn't afford to replace them so Tamika had to learn how to adapt. She worked harder to compensate, becoming good at reading lips, and picking up tiny nuances in body language.

Tamika inherited her family's passion for basketball and practiced at every opportunity. On the court she found that her hearing loss helped her. She might not hear her teammates, but being able to read subtle shifts in body language was invaluable. She could anticipate her opponent's moves and see where she was needed. The basketball court was where she excelled, and felt safe and accepted.

"One day I'll be in the NBA." That was Tamika's goal. She wrote it down and pinned it to the bathroom mirror. Her parents didn't tell her this was an impossible dream. They didn't tell her that no girl had played in the NBA before. Instead they supported her. Tamika worked hard. She was on the court before anybody else and stayed after everyone had gone home.

As women's basketball grew in popularity the WNBA league was formed in 1996. Tamika was signed by Indiana Fever, who she stayed with for her entire career. After a disappointing first year spent recovering from injury, she was soon back to fighting form and enjoyed a spectacular career. They advanced to the playoffs 13 times and won the WNBA title in 2012. Tamika was also called up to represent team USA. Her first Olympic Games was Athens 2004, where she won the gold medal. This set a trend for the next three Games, which she followed up with golds in Beijing 2008, London 2012, and Rio 2016. She is one of the few basketballers in the world to win four Olympic gold medals.

"WE HAVE AN OPPORTUNITY TO HAVE AN IMPACT."

FIGHT *like a* GIRL
Katheryn Winnick

Full name: **Katerena Anna Vinitska**
Sports: **Taekwondo and karate**
Birth date: **December 17, 1977**
Place of birth: **Etobicoke, Ontario, Canada**
Best achievements: **Third-degree black belt and award-winning actress**

Did you know...?

★ On the set of *Vikings* she taught self-defense classes to her female co-stars. Katheryn is passionate about inspiring girls to have courage and confidence, and feels that teaching them self-defense is important for empowerment.

★ Katheryn is a licensed bodyguard, third-degree black belt in taekwondo, and second-degree black belt in karate.

★ Katheryn can speak five different languages. Ukrainian is her first language and she also speaks English, Russian, French, and Italian.

Katheryn Winnick is best known for her award-winning career as an actor. She has played some fierce characters in TV and film, but sport has underpinned her rise to success. An expert martial artist, she is skilled in combat and can hold her own against the toughest opponents.

When Katheryn was seven her parents decided to do taekwondo as a family. In the dojo she found her passion. She trained for four hours a day and six years later Katheryn earned her black belt. From there she began to teach her skills to others. What started as an after-school program turned into a blossoming business, and at 16 Katheryn opened her first martial arts school.

Katheryn competed nationally and was ranked second in Canada, but chose to turn down the opportunity to try for the Olympic Games. A big decision, but Katheryn wanted to focus on her university career. She completed a degree in kinesiology at York University (Ontario), opening another two martial arts schools while she was studying.

It was sport that led Katheryn into acting. She taught martial arts to actors and worked as a stunt double on movie sets.

This gave her a real understanding of what went on behind the camera, and she loved the challenges and creativity that the industry offered. Katheryn decided to go for a career change. She went to acting school in New York and took every part she could get to gain experience and exposure. It was not easy, but Katheryn was determined that she was going to make it.

Her most famous role to date is that of the shield maiden Lagertha in the TV series *Vikings*. A powerful warrior queen who is unbeatable on the battlefield, Lagertha is confident, tough, and fearless, just like Katheryn. This role was very physically demanding, but she loved being able to bring her martial arts experience to it. Fighting with a sword and shield was different to punching and kicking, but Katheryn applied the same mentality she brought to her sport and performed many of her own stunts.

"PLAN AND PREPARE, BUT WHEN THE TIME COMES TRUST YOURSELF AND LET GO."

REFEREE *like a* GIRL
Stéphanie Frappart

Full name: **Stéphanie Frappart**
Sport: **Soccer**
Birth date: **December 14, 1983**
Place of birth: **Herblay-sur-Seine, France**
Best achievement: **First woman to officiate a major men's European match**

Did you know...?

★ Stéphanie refereed two women's games in the Rio 2016 Olympics, giving out four yellow cards and one red.

★ Training to be a referee is intense. Stéphanie started working towards the 2019 World Cup back in 2015, attending seminars and workshops as well as keeping on top of the physical fitness requirements.

★ When Stéphanie refereed her first Ligue 1 match, commentators openly admitted that they watched her carefully to see whether she slipped up. If they were looking to find fault they were disappointed as she showed her knowledge, talent, and skill on the pitch.

Without a dedicated stream of volunteers, coaches, and officials, sport as we know it would not exist. We hear about awesome athletes, but often the team behind the team goes unrecognized. Every official has a backstory and Stéphanie Frappart is a trailblazer in her field, paving the path for other young women to forge a career of their choosing in sport.

Stéphanie played soccer for FC Parisis, a small club to the north of Paris. At 13 she developed an interest in the rules of the game and started to referee local matches. It didn't take long for this new passion to grow and Stéphanie found herself playing less and less. She decided to focus on refereeing full-time when she was 18. There were very few female referees to learn from, but that didn't put Stéphanie off. She kept studying the game and putting her name forward. In 2009 she was added to the FIFA International Referee List.

Soccer players can get stroppy if a decision goes against them, an emotion that is often mirrored by fans. It's important for referees to be decisive and hold their ground. They also need to be really fit, and Stéphanie runs between six to eight miles in a match. Referees must pass a fitness test as well as undertaking strict training to prove that they are physically, tactically, and technically competent. There are no concessions made for Stéphanie because she is female, nor does she want there to be.

In 2014 Stéphanie became the first woman to referee in Ligue 2, the second tier of professional soccer in France. In 2019 she progressed to Ligue 1 and refereed the women's World Cup final.

History was also made when she was appointed as referee for the UEFA Super Cup. She became the first woman to officiate a major men's European match, and led a team of predominantly female officials. With only two Ligue 1 matches under her belt some critics questioned whether she had the experience. FIFA backed up their decision, as did her male colleagues, and she and her team delivered a strong performance. She has gone on to be the first woman to referee games in the World Cup qualifying rounds and the Champions League, and the Coupe de France final.

"THE PLAYERS DON'T RUN SLOWER BECAUSE I AM REFEREEING SO THE PHYSICAL REQUIREMENTS MUST BE THE SAME FOR EVERYBODY."

PLAY *like a* GIRL
Serena Williams

Serena Williams is a sporting legend who has achieved world domination like no other. Her presence on the court and her drive to win makes her a formidable opponent who has raised the bar in tennis.

Serena grew up in an area where gangs roamed the streets and the sound of gunfire was normal. She started playing tennis with her family when she was three. Her parents couldn't afford a junior racket so she played with a full-sized one, which was almost as big as her. Serena and her four sisters played at the local tennis courts after school for two hours every day, and as they got older this increased. They worked hard, practicing drills, playing competitive games, and preparing to be winners.

Serena entered her first professional competition when she was 14, and she lost spectacularly. She wanted to come back better and stronger, so she worked hard behind the scenes to up her game. A year later she returned to the tournament scene and finished the season ranked 99th in the world. She was 16. Her first Grand Slam win came two years later at the US Open. Grand Slams are the most prestigious tennis tournaments in the world and she became the second African American to win one. At Wimbledon in 2002 she went through the entire tournament without dropping a set, beating her sister Venus, the top seed, in the final.

Her career hasn't jumped from one success to another, but has been hard fought and well deserved. Serena has recovered from multiple injuries and surgeries. She survived a life-threatening illness that took her a year to recover from. Every loss at a competition only fueled her hunger to win. It is this fire that has seen her transcend any other tennis player, woman or man, to win 23 Grand Slam singles and four Olympic titles. She has won all four Grand Slams in a row twice, a feat the papers called the Serena Slam.

Through it all, family remain important. While Venus is her biggest rival, she is also her best friend and Serena says that she'd not be the competitor she is today without her.

"YOU HAVE TO BELIEVE IN YOURSELF WHEN NO ONE ELSE DOES."

Did you know...?

Serena has teamed up with her sister Venus in the doubles, winning 14 Grand Slam doubles titles together. They have also won gold medals in the doubles in the 2000, 2008, and 2012 Olympic Games.

Serena won the Australian Open while eight weeks pregnant, but was very ill after giving birth to her daughter. She spent six weeks unable to get out of bed, but eight months later she played in the French Open.

Serena launched her own clothing line with the mission of helping women feel confident about the way they look.

Full name: **Serena Jameka Williams**
Sport: **Tennis**
Birth date: **September 26, 1981**
Place of birth: **Saginaw, Michigan, USA**
Team: **USA**
Best achievements: **23 Grand Slam singles wins and four Olympic gold medals**

MULTITALENTED *like a* GIRL
Oksana Masters

Full name: **Oksana Alexandrovna Masters**
Sports: **Rowing, cycling, biathlon, and skiing**
Birth date: **June 19, 1989**
Place of birth: **Khmelnytskyi, Ukraine**
Team: **USA**
Best achievement: **Seventeen Paralympic medals in four different sports**

Did you know...?

★ Oksana is always up for a new challenge. Around her training she fits in fun activities like rock climbing, abseiling, kayaking, and paddleboarding.

★ An elbow fracture three weeks before PyeongChang and a fall during the Games forced Oksana to pull out of a race. She had to dig deep into her reserves to find the strength to keep going, returning to the snow to win her gold medals.

★ Oksana went back to Ukraine and spoke to children in orphanages. She is thankful for her second chance and wants to show other children that no matter where you come from it is possible to succeed.

"NEVER LET SOCIETY DETERMINE WHAT YOU SEE WHEN YOU LOOK IN THE MIRROR."

Most athletes focus on one sport. Not Oksana Masters. This girl takes the word talented to a whole new level. She has represented her country in four different sports, winning medals in all of them.

Oksana was born three years after the Chernobyl nuclear power plant disaster. Radiation drifted across Europe and many babies were affected by it. Oksana was born with one kidney, five fingers on each hand, six toes on each foot, and she was missing bones in her legs. Her birth family couldn't afford to give her the right medical support so Oksana lived in an orphanage. She dreamed of being adopted by a loving family, and when she was seven she finally got her wish. Her adoptive mother took her to live with her in America. This wasn't an easy adjustment. Oksana had to learn to speak English, and the severity of her disability meant that both her legs needed amputating.

Oksana decided to try rowing when she was 13. The freedom she felt out on the water was indescribable and it helped Oksana channel some of the painful memories of her early childhood. What started as a hobby evolved into a career, and she met fellow amputee Rob Jones in 2011. They trained hard together and the following year they won the bronze medal in the double sculls in the London 2012 Paralympic Games.

Oksana was looking for big results at the 2013 World Championships. However, a back injury flared up in the middle of the competition and surgeons were unable to repair the damage. Oksana was told that her rowing career was over. Not being able to take part in sport was excruciating, and she was determined to find another one. She tried cross-country skiing, and in an incredibly quick turnaround, Oksana made the Paralympic team for Sochi 2014 where she won a silver and a bronze!

Oksana decided to try hand-cycling to improve her strength and fitness for skiing. Two years later she competed in Rio 2016, finishing fourth in the road race and fifth in the time trial, before winning gold in both events in Tokyo 2020. As if this wasn't enough, Oksana picked up a fourth sport: the biathlon. This combines cross-country skiing with rifle shooting. At the Winter Paralympics in PyeongChang 2018 Oksana won two golds and a bronze in cross-country skiing, and a silver and bronze in the biathlon, while she went even better in Beijing 2022, winning two golds in the biathlon and one in cross-country skiing.

Chrissie Wellington

Full name: **Christine Ann Wellington OBE**
Sport: **Ironman triathlon**
Birth date: **February 18, 1977**
Place of birth: **Bury St Edmunds, Suffolk, UK**
Team: **Great Britain**
Best achievement: **Four-time world champion**

Did you know...?

★ Chrissie spent 16 months living in Nepal where she helped to improve water, sanitation, and health in a district affected by conflict. She explored the countryside on a mountain bike, cycling across the Himalayas to Everest base camp.

★ Chrissie holds the world record for the Ironman distance triathlon: 8 hours, 18 minutes, 13 seconds, and regularly finished before many of the elite men.

★ In 2012 Chrissie came across a local parkrun and loved the concept so much that she joined the team, becoming Global Head of Health and Wellbeing. Parkruns are free, accessible, community-led events that everyone can take part in, and she is proud to help people become happier and healthier.

As a child, Chrissie Wellington did quite a bit of swimming, but she didn't take it too seriously. Her studies came first and she wasn't going to let anything get in the way of good exam results. Two years of traveling after university helped her understand her passions better and she decided to pursue a career in international development, doing a master's degree and getting a job as a policy advisor to the government.

In her early 20s Chrissie decided to start running. The London Marathon was her first big event, which she ran in 2002 to raise money for charity. The buzz she got left her wanting to do more, but after injuring her leg she returned to swimming to stay fit. It was then that a friend suggested she try a triathlon. Chrissie always likes to seize every opportunity, so she decided to throw herself into this new challenge.

Chrissie learned how to mount and dismount her bike properly the day before the Shropshire Triathlon. She won the event, qualifying for the World Championships in Lausanne, Switzerland. Determined to give this her best shot Chrissie asked a coach to help her and trained hard. She hoped for a top ten finish, but won her age group and was the fastest woman overall. Now crowned world champion as an amateur, she made the decision to turn professional. Giving up her job was a big risk, but if she didn't give this her all she knew she would never uncover her true potential.

Her coach asked whether she wanted to try an Ironman. This is one of the toughest events in the world, pushing human endurance to the very limits. It starts with a 2.4-mile (3.8km) swim, followed by a 112-mile (180km) bike ride, and finishes with a marathon. It requires athletes to be physically prepared, mentally strong, and able to overcome self-doubt and discomfort. The first time Chrissie attempted this event she finished 50 minutes ahead of her competitors. In doing so she qualified for the World Ironman Championships. Making the start line in your first year as a professional athlete is an impressive feat, but Chrissie went better than that and won the World Championship title, retaining it in 2008, 2009, and 2011.

"HARD WORK AND AN OPEN MIND IS THE ONLY WAY TO REALIZE THE POTENTIAL THAT IS INSIDE EVERY ONE OF US."

STRONG *like a* GIRL
Lydia Valentín

Full name: **Lydia Valentín Pérez**
Sport: **Weightlifting**
Birth date: **February 10, 1985**
Place of birth: **Ponferrada, Spain**
Team: **Spain**
Best achievement: **Olympic gold medalist**

Did you know...?

★ Lydia is super-strong. She competes in the 75kg weight category and her personal best is 124kg in the snatch, and 147kg in the clean and jerk.

★ It can take a long time for drug cheats like those she competed with to be brought to justice. Samples are stored for up to ten years and can be retested when better techniques become available.

★ She won the World Championships in 2017 and 2018, and a silver in 2019. She has also won the European Championships four times.

Sport requires a lot of patience. Weightlifter Lydia Valentín knows this better than most. She has three Olympic medals, but has only got to stand on the podium once.

An exceptional gymnast, fast runner, and gifted basketballer, as a child Lydia was brimming with sporting potential. Coach Álvarez knew these talents would stand her in good stead for weightlifting and when she was 11 he invited her to try it. Lydia was curious at first, and over time that curiosity turned into passion. Three years later she was national champion.

Her achievements earned her the opportunity to train with the national team full time. This was a big decision. Lydia was only 15 and the training center was 250 miles (402km) away from her home. Weightlifting was her dream, and she knew this was the right choice. It would allow her to take her sport as far as she could. Training full time was tough on her body, but Lydia kept persevering when those around her quit. The harder she trained, the stronger she got and soon she was representing her country.

Lydia won medals at European and World Championships, but one at the Olympics proved elusive. She placed fifth in Beijing 2008 and fourth in London 2012. Days before she competed in Rio 2016 the International Olympic Committee announced that all three medalists in London 2012 had been caught taking performance-enhancing substances. They were stripped of their medals, and Lydia's fourth place was upgraded to gold.

This was a great way to start a Games, and it only got better. Lydia lifted a total of 257kg in Rio to win bronze. A few days later she learned she had won another medal. More retesting showed that another three athletes had failed their drugs test in Beijing 2008, and she was retrospectively awarded silver.

While Lydia eventually received her medals, the memory of standing on top of the podium at an Olympics cannot be replaced. Nor can the lost sponsorship opportunities that often accompany an Olympic win. This is not the reason that athletes do sport, but it certainly makes life easier and is undermined when others cheat their way to success.

"ALL MY LIFE I HAVE COMPETED AGAINST PEOPLE WHO DON'T PLAY BY THE RULES."

JOUST *like a* GIRL

Sarah Hay

T-shirt, leggings, and sneakers are the items that normally make up an athlete's kit, but Sarah Hay wears a suit of armor. She is a modern-day lady knight, a fearless jouster who rides into combat with her visor down and her shield up.

Jousting was popular in medieval times. Arenas would fill with people eager to watch knights charging at each other on horseback. Their raised lances would clatter against each other's shield, which was no mean feat when galloping at full pelt. Winners were decided on how hard they hit, shattering their lances and sometimes unseating their opponent.

There has been a resurgence of interest in jousting in recent years. The rules are largely the same, where the competitors make three passes against their opponent and try to hit them as effectively as possible with their lance. While the medieval game was primarily a sport for noblemen, women are now allowed to take part, and they all compete against one another.

Sarah is head teacher, not a knight, by trade, and didn't try jousting until she was 37. Sarah first saw jousting at a medieval re-enactment in the Blue Mountains, Australia. She was hooked and found herself a trainer. She had ridden horses competitively in the past but she now had to learn how to do it one-handed, while balancing a lance and shield, and wearing a 77lb (35kg) suit of armor.

Sarah favors accuracy over strength. At 5ft 5in (1.65m), she is smaller than many of her competitors, but her deadly aim and skill at horse riding is a winning combination. At her first international competition in Belgium she beat the European champion and won the sport joust trophy. From there she traveled the world to joust, racking up an impressive win count. In 2018 she became the first woman to win the Queen's Jubilee Horn at the Royal Armouries in Leeds.

Even with armor she has had a few injuries, including broken bones and concussion. She was once hit so hard that she almost got knocked off her horse. As soon as she recovered she was back competing and Sarah doesn't think she will retire until she is at least 60.

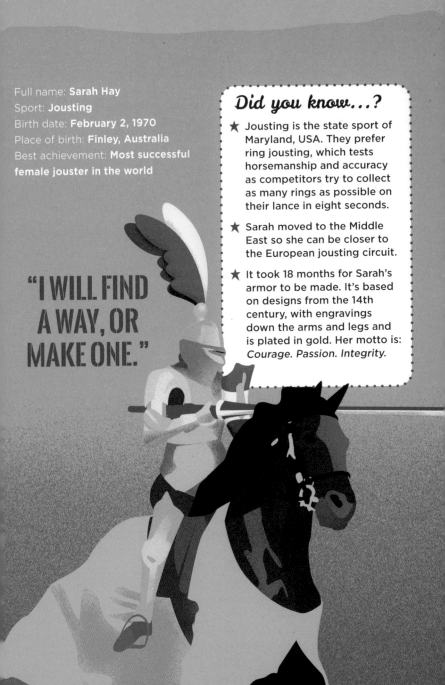

Full name: **Sarah Hay**
Sport: **Jousting**
Birth date: **February 2, 1970**
Place of birth: **Finley, Australia**
Best achievement: **Most successful female jouster in the world**

"I WILL FIND A WAY, OR MAKE ONE."

Did you know...?

★ Jousting is the state sport of Maryland, USA. They prefer ring jousting, which tests horsemanship and accuracy as competitors try to collect as many rings as possible on their lance in eight seconds.

★ Sarah moved to the Middle East so she can be closer to the European jousting circuit.

★ It took 18 months for Sarah's armor to be made. It's based on designs from the 14th century, with engravings down the arms and legs and is plated in gold. Her motto is: *Courage. Passion. Integrity.*

RISE TO THE TOP *like a* GIRL
Saina Nehwal

Full name: **Saina Nehwal**
Sport: **Badminton**
Birth date: **March 17, 1990**
Place of birth: **Hisar, Haryana, India**
Team: **India**
Best achievement: **World number one**

Did you know...?

Before badminton became her favorite sport Saina trained for a year in karate, progressing quickly to earn her brown belt.

Saina has won over 43 international medals, and become one of the highest-paid badminton players in the world.

Saina is an ambassador for the Save The Girl Child campaign. She is passionate about encouraging more girls to take part in sport, sharing her story to change the idea that it is a profession for men.

"YOU CAN'T LET THE HIGHS MAKE YOU FEEL OVERCONFIDENT, NOR CAN YOU LET THE LOWS BE A REASON TO DAMPEN YOUR SPIRIT."

Hard work sits at the core of Saina Nehwal's success. The time she commits to her training has seen her rise to become one of the best badminton players in the world, and in doing so she has redefined what it means to play like a girl.

In Haryana, the state Saina comes from, some families believe that having a girl is a curse, and her grandmother was disappointed that Saina was not a boy. Her parents had no such prejudices and were determined that Saina and her sister were given every opportunity to succeed in life. She tried lots of sports, but didn't pick up a badminton racket until she was eight. Her father got promoted at work so the Nehwal family moved over 1,000 miles (1,610km) away to Hyderabad. They speak a different language there and Saina went to a badminton summer camp to try to make friends.

When it became clear that Saina was talented at badminton she started training more seriously, but it was expensive. Her father took money from his pension fund and borrowed from friends and family to pay for it. Saina repaid him by working hard. The training facility was 15 miles (24km) away so she'd get up at 4am every morning. After a two-hour session she would rush to school, then head back to the training center when her classes finished. This regime was hard, but walking away was never an option. She had fallen in love with the game.

When she is out on the court it is all about one thing for Saina: winning. And this is something she excels at. She won silver at the Commonwealth Youth Games and gold at the Junior World Championships. At 16 she was the youngest player from Asia to win a 4-star tournament. She went in seeded 86th and came out with the title. At the 2010 Commonwealth Games in Delhi she won a gold medal and at London 2012 she took the bronze. Her continued success saw her rise to world number one. India started to pay attention. Badminton traditionally fell under the radar, but Saina's achievements raised its profile. Coming from a place where being a girl was seen as a burden, Saina has changed people's perceptions of what girls can achieve.

ADVENTURE *like a* GIRL
Mollie Hughes

Did you know...?

★ Mollie raised money for Cancer Research on her second Everest adventure. Her aim was to get £8,848 (about US$12,000), £1 for every 3ft (1m) of Everest.

★ Mollie crossed the Jordan desert in 2018 with Cal Major and Bex Band. They hiked the 125 miles (200km) in sweltering heat carrying all their equipment.

★ When you're exercising it's important to replace the calories you burn. During her expedition to the South Pole Mollie was eating 4,500 calories per day but still lost 22lb (10kg).

Full name: **Mollie Hughes**
Sport: **Adventuring**
Birth date: **July 3, 1990**
Place of birth: **London, UK**
Best achievement: **Youngest woman to reach the South Pole solo**

Only by stepping out of your comfort zone can you access your true potential. Mollie Hughes knows that the mind is stronger than the body, and with enough resilience you can reach the top of the world.

Mollie's passion for mountaineering started on a school trip to Africa where she got the chance to climb Mount Kenya. At university she wrote her dissertation about Mount Everest. Studying sport psychology, she was interested in the mental approach of conquering one of the world's toughest mountains. As she learned more about Everest, Mollie knew she had to experience it for herself. At 21 she successfully reached the top in a two-month expedition. This adventure taught Mollie a lot about herself. Growing up she was shy, but proving to herself that she could achieve something this big gave her more confidence.

Five years later Mollie was back on Everest, this time attempting to break a record. If she made it up the north side she would become the youngest woman to summit the mountain from both sides. This route brings different challenges: it's colder, windier, and you spend more time in the Death Zone. Above 26,000ft (8,000m) oxygen is very low, and the human body cannot survive for long. Mollie successfully stood on the summit for a second time on May 16, 2017, just as the sun came up.

Records are there to be broken and in 2019 Mollie set her sights on another: a solo mission to the South Pole. She set off from the west coast of Antarctica and skied 702 miles (1,130km) across some of the most inhospitable terrain on the planet, dragging her 230lb (105kg) supply sled behind her. With temperatures dropping to –58°F (–50°C), hazardous crevasse fields to navigate, and living on freeze-dried food, this was not going to be an easy journey.

She hoped to reach the South Pole on New Year's Day but challenging conditions in the first couple of weeks put her behind schedule. For eight days Mollie was stuck in a blizzard, unable to see more than 3ft (1m) in front of her. It took her 59 days to reach the South Pole from start to finish. Only 23 other people have successfully managed this route solo and Mollie became the youngest woman to do so at the age of 29.

"I'M NOT EXTRAORDINARY. I'VE SIMPLY ADJUSTED MY MINDSET TO BELIEVE I COULD ACHIEVE SOMETHING EXTRAORDINARY."

SLIDE *like a* GIRL
Lizzy Yarnold

Speeding head-first down an icy track on a small sled, taking bends at 80 miles per hour (129km/h), requires a certain amount of fearlessness. Skeleton athlete Lizzy Yarnold is a fierce competitor who shows that there is no place for quitters when you're going for gold.

Watching Denise Lewis win gold in Sydney 2000 inspired Lizzy to set her sights on the Olympics. She took up heptathlon and wasn't bad at it either, making it as far as regional level.

Eight years later she attended a Girls4Gold talent program with 900 other promising athletes, each one hoping that coaches would see their potential to win a medal for their country. The staff identified Lizzy as a promising skeleton athlete.

Within three years Lizzy had won medals at the junior and senior World Championships. What makes Lizzy's story even more impressive is that there isn't a skeleton track in the UK, so she can't practice sliding for nine months of the year. In competition athletes are only allowed six practice runs to get used to the course. Many of Lizzy's competitors live close to skeleton tracks and get the opportunity to train all year round, so she had to be a quick learner and make every run count.

Her first Winter Olympics was Sochi 2014. Lizzy dominated the competition right from the first run, and maintained a solid lead. That dream of becoming Olympic Champion came true.

After this Lizzy took a year off. Taking time out to look after herself and regain her focus gave her the best shot of retaining her Olympic title. But her run up to the next Olympics was not a smooth ride.

Before PyeongChang 2018 she had been struggling with dizzy spells, which is not ideal when you're hurtling around corners at frightening speeds. To make matters worse Lizzy had come down with a bad chest infection in the middle of the Olympics. She was struggling to breathe and felt so ill she thought she might have to pull out. Her physiotherapist encouraged her to keep going and on the final run Lizzy broke the track record to take the lead and win her second Olympic gold.

Full name: **Elizabeth Anne Yarnold OBE**
Sport: **Skeleton**
Birth date: **October 31, 1988**
Place of birth: **Sevenoaks, Kent, UK**
Team: **Great Britain**
Best achievement: **Two-time Olympic gold medalist**

"IT'S IMPORTANT TO KNOW HOW TO WIN AND IT'S ALSO VERY IMPORTANT TO KNOW HOW TO FAIL."

BE THE BEST *like a girl*
Rachel Atherton

Full name: **Rachel Laura Atherton**
Sport: **Mountain biking**
Birth date: **December 6, 1987**
Place of birth: **Salisbury, UK**
Team: **Great Britain**
Best achievements: **14 consecutive World Cup wins and five-time world champion**

Did you know...?

★ The Atherton siblings, Rachel, Dan, and Gee, have their own bike company. Atherton Bikes uses 3D printing to make mountain bikes fully customizable.

★ They have also opened Dyfi Bike Park where people can ride Dan's trails. Rachel often works at the park, leading coaching sessions with local children. She is passionate about getting girls to try racing.

★ The rainbow jersey can only be worn by a reigning world champion. It is white with five colored bands and Rachel likes to keep hers in a birdcage.

Rachel Atherton has earned the reputation as the greatest downhill racer of all time, and justifiably so. With 39 World Cup wins to her name, she has revolutionized the mountain biking world and helped grow an outside sport into a popular pastime.

Rachel's brother Dan did BMX. Their father took him to races at the weekend and it didn't take long before Dan had persuaded Rachel and brother Gee to join him. For eight-year-old Rachel, competing was far more fun than supporting from the sidelines and three years later the family got involved with mountain biking. Rachel wasn't just good at this. She was exceptional.

Rachel moved to Wales in her teens. This is the perfect location for mountain biking, boasting some spectacular tracks. She put in the practice, supported by her brother Dan who has a talent for building challenging tracks. The best bit about mountain biking for Rachel is racing. She loves testing herself against the course, throwing all her focus into getting everything right. And she loves to go fast. To get the results on race day Rachel must train hard and her efforts paid off. At 16 she won the British Senior National Championships, a win that set her up for world domination.

In 2008 Rachel won her first World Championships, shortly followed by a World Cup title. Getting to the top is one thing. Staying there is more difficult, but Rachel made it look easy. Between 2015 and 2017 she achieved something that had never been done before: she won 14 World Cup events in a row as well as the World Championships. This impressive run came to an end when she dislocated her shoulder in training at the UK round of the 2017 World Cup Series, forcing her to pull out of the competition. A few months later Rachel broke her collarbone at the World Championships.

Rachel's hunger to return to the competition circuit drove her to work hard on her rehabilitation. It takes courage to keep pursuing a goal that could result in another injury, but when Rachel is on the bike she knows she is doing what she is meant to do. The following year she was back in fighting form, winning the World Championships at Val di Sole, Italy, and coming first overall in the World Cup.

"SPORT GIVES YOU SUCH A GOOD FEELING AND MAKES YOU FEEL STRONG INSIDE. I THINK EVERY GIRL SHOULD HAVE THAT OPPORTUNITY."

ABOUT *the* AUTHOR
Danielle Brown

Did you know...?

★ Danielle studied law at university, juggling it with her training to graduate with first class honors.

★ Danielle is the first disabled athlete to represent England on the able-bodied team. At the 2010 Commonwealth Games she won a gold medal in the team event.

★ A rule change after London 2012 means that she can no longer compete at the Paralympics. This was tough, but she now inspires young people to dream big, break barriers, and feel confident.

Full name: **Danielle Elizabeth Brown MBE**
Sport: **Archery**
Birth date: **April 10, 1988**
Place of birth: **Steeton, Yorkshire, UK**
Team: **Great Britain**
Best achievements: **Two Paralympic gold medals and five-time world champion**

Danielle has always loved sport, but she wasn't naturally gifted at it. Her younger sisters used to beat her at running. When she tried kayaking she got a certificate to say she'd achieved more swimming than canoeing. And she was not a fast swimmer. This didn't matter. Sport for Danielle wasn't a career plan, it was a way to have fun, meet friends, and stay active.

When she was 11 Danielle's feet started to hurt. It wasn't a big deal to start with, but the pain got worse and worse. Soon she was struggling to walk and couldn't take part in the sports she loved. Five years later Danielle was diagnosed with Complex Regional Pain Syndrome (CRPS). Instead of focusing on what she couldn't do, Danielle looked at what she could. She might not be able to run any more, but that didn't mean she couldn't still do sport.

On her 15th birthday she started archery with her father. Danielle spent most of her time picking arrows off the ground not the target, but she found it so much fun. Every night she'd pester her parents to take her training. The more she practiced the better she got, the better she got the more she enjoyed it, and the more she wanted to practice. Three years later Danielle made the Great Britain team, jumping straight in as world number one. She held this position for the rest of her international career.

At the Beijing 2008 Paralympic Games she started the competition with a world record. It was all looking great, but the night before the semi-finals she felt anxious. What if she couldn't do it tomorrow? What if she let herself down? After reading inspirational words from her support team, Danielle went out and beat both opponents by a convincing margin, taking gold at her first Games. She also learned that if she wanted to keep winning she had to believe in herself and her ability no matter what. When she got home Danielle spent a lot of time working on her confidence levels. As it got bigger, so did her results: world records, world firsts, world titles, and another gold medal in London 2012.

"EVEN IN ADVERSITY WE HAVE A CHOICE: TO GET UP OR TO GIVE UP."

INDEX

A

abseiling 92
acting 86, 87
activism 18, 24, 25, 53, 68, 76, 79, 80, 100
Adams, Nicola 32–33
Adams, Valerie 42–43
adoption 30, 93
adventuring 58–59, 82–83, 102–103
Alphonsi, Maggie 44–45
amputation 39, 75, 93
archery 108–109
army 48, 62, 63
asthma 54
Atherton, Rachel 106–107
athletics 8–9, 26–27, 66–67, 70–71
attitude 45, 61, 75

B

badminton 100–101
ballet 20, 36–37
basketball 84–85, 96
   wheelchair 20–21
biathlon 92, 93
Biles, Simone 30–31
body shaming 64
boxing 32–33
brain damage 20
Brown, Danielle 108–109
Brown, Sky 72–73
bullying 64, 85

C

cancer 24, 43, 46, 66, 67, 102
Carr, Lizzie 24–25
Catchings, Tamika 84–85

cerebral palsy 69
Christiansen, Sophie 68–69
coaching 40–41
Cockroft, Hannah 20–21
Cooke, Liv 22–23
Copeland, Misty 36–37
Cox, Lynne 28–29
cricket 10–11, 41,
cycling 54–55, 58, 59, 94 82–83, 92–93

D

dancing 20, 36–37
Darke, Karen 82–83
degree 8, 18, 24, 40
   master's 58, 68, 95
DiGiulian, Sasha 64–65
disability 21, 68, 75, 83, 93
doping 31, 43, 56, 57, 96, 97
dressage 69
du Toit, Natalie 74–75

E

Ennis-Hill, Jessica 70–71

F

failure 62, 65
Felix, Allyson 8–9
fencing 76–77
Feng, Shanshan 60–61
Fitzpatrick, Menna 48–49
football 22–23, 41, 50–51, 88–89
Formula One 18, 19
Frappart, Stéphanie 88–89

G

golf 60–61
gymnastics 30–31

H

Hamblin, Nikki 26–27
Hamilton, Bethany 12–13
Hay, Sarah 98–99
hearing loss 85
heptathlon 70–71, 104
high jump 56–57, 70
hiking 24, 59, 102
hockey
   field 16–17
   ice 34–35
horse riding 24, 68–69, 98–99
Hughes, Mollie 102–103

I

injury 9, 17, 22, 27, 45, 48, 70, 71, 85, 90, 93, 95, 107

J

jousting 98–99

K

karate 86–87, 100
karting 18
kayaking 83, 92, 109
Kenny, Laura 54–55

L

Lasitskene, Mariya 56–57

M

MacArthur, Ellen 78–79
Mardini, Yusra 52–53
Marta 50–51
martial arts 86–87
Masters, Oksana 92–93
motherhood 13, 42, 46, 47, 55, 71, 76
motorsport 18–19
mountain biking 94,

106–107
mountaineering 38–39, 64–65, 102–103
music 14, 37, 45

N
Nehwal, Saina 100–101
netball 40–41
Neville, Tracey 40–41

O
Olympic Games 9, 16, 17, 26, 27, 30, 31, 32, 33, 34, 43, 50, 52, 53, 54, 55, 56, 61, 62, 63, 66, 67, 70, 71, 73, 74, 75, 76, 77, 80, 81, 85, 87, 88, 91, 95, 97, 101, 104, 105

P
paddleboarding 24–25, 92
para equestrian 68–69
Paralympic Games 21, 48, 69, 75, 82, 83, 93, 108, 109
passion 7
pentathlon 70
PhD 46, 82
pregnancy 9, 42, 46, 70, 91
premature birth 54, 69

R
refereeing 88–89
refugee 52, 53
Rhéaume, Manon 34–35
Richardson-Walsh, Kate 16–17
rock climbing 64–65, 82, 83, 92
rowing 62–63, 92–93
rugby union 44–45

running 8–9, 19, 26–27, 66, 95, 109
cross-country 80
fell 46–47
marathon 58, 59, 80–81, 95

S
sailing 78–79
self-confidence 7, 31, 35, 51, 69, 80, 86, 103, 108, 109
shark attack 12, 13
shot put 42–43
Sinha, Arunima 38–39
skating 72–73
skeleton 104–105
skiing
adaptive 83
alpine 48–49
cross-country 92–93
soccer 22–23, 41, 50–51, 88–89
squash 14–15
Stanning, Heather 26, 62–63
success 7, 20, 41, 48, 63, 76, 90, 97, 101
surfing 12–13, 73
swimming 52–53, 74–75, 95, 109
open-water 28–29
Switzer, Kathrine 80–81

T
taekwondo 86–87
talent 6, 7
Taylor, Sarah 10–11
tennis 90–91
Toorpakai, Maria 14–15
track and field 8–9, 58, 66–67

triathlon
Ironman 94–95
para- 82

U
university 8, 18, 24, 35, 45, 46, 47, 63, 64, 65, 68, 70, 80, 84, 87, 95, 103, 108

V
Valentín, Lydia 96–97
Vezzali, Valentina 76–77
Vieira da Silva, Marta 50–51
visual impairment 48

W
war 29, 53, 76
weightlifting 96–97
Wellington, Chrissie 94–95
wheelchair racing 20–21
Williams, Sarah 58–59
Williams, Serena 90–91
Williams-Mills, Novlene 66–67
Winnick, Katheryn 86–87
Winter Olympic Games 34, 104
Winter Paralympic Games 48, 49, 92, 93
Wolff, Susie 18–19
writing 64

Y
Yarnold, Lizzie 104–105

This edition published 2022 by Button Books, an imprint of
Guild of Master Craftsman Publications Ltd
Castle Place, 166 High Street, Lewes,
East Sussex BN7 1XU, UK

First edition published 2021

Text © Danielle Brown, 2021
Copyright in the Work © GMC Publications Ltd, 2021

ISBN 978 1 78708 127 7

Distributed by Publishers Group West in the United States.

A catalog record for this book is available from the British Library.

Publisher Jonathan Bailey
Production Jim Bulley
Editor Wendy McAngus
Design & Illustration Robin Shields

Color origination by GMC Reprographics
Printed and bound in China

For more on Button Books, contact:
GMC Publications Ltd, Castle Place,
166 High Street, Lewes, East Sussex,
BN7 1XU, United Kingdom
Tel: +44 (0)1273 488005
buttonbooks.co.uk
buttonbooks.us